# stress
# buster

Summersdale Publishers Ltd
46 West Street
Chichester
West Sussex
PO19 1RP

www.summersdale.com

www.geoffthompson.com

Printed and bound in Great Britain.

ISBN 1 84024 509 3

Cartoons by John Smyth

geoff thompson

# stress buster

## how to stop stress from killing you

## About the Author

Geoff Thompson claims that his biological birthdate is 1960, though his hair-line goes right back to the First World War.

He has worked as a floor sweeper, chemical worker, pizza maker, road digger, hod-carrier, martial arts instructor, bricklayer, picture seller, delivery driver and nightclub bouncer before giving up 'proper work' in 1992 to write full time.

He is now a bestselling author, BAFTA-winning screenwriter, magazine columnist, playwright and novelist.

He lives in Coventry with his wife Sharon.

www.geoffthompson.com

## Other books and DVDs
## by Geoff Thompson

*Books:*

Red Mist

Watch My Back: The Geoff Thompson Autobiography

The Elephant and the Twig: The Art of Positive Thinking

The Great Escape: The 10 Secrets to Loving Your Life and Living Your Dreams

Fear – The Friend of Exceptional People: Techniques in Controlling Fear

Shape Shifter: Transform Your Life in 1 Day

The Formula: The Secret to a Better Life

Real Grappling

Real Punching

Real Kicking

Real Head, Knees and Elbows

Dead or Alive: The Choice is Yours

Three Second Fighter: The Sniper Option

Weight Training: For the Martial Artist

The Pavement Arena: Adapting Combat Martial Arts to the Street

Animal Day: Pressure Testing the Martial Arts

The Fence: The Art of Protection

The Art of Fighting Without Fighting

The Throws and Takedowns of Judo

The Throws and Takedowns of Sombo Russian Wrestling

The Throws and Takedowns of Freestyle Wrestling

The Throws and Takedowns of Greco-Roman Wrestling

*The Ground Fighting Series*

Pins: The Bedrock

The Escapes

Chokes and Strangles

Arm Bars and Joint Locks

Fighting From Your Back

Fighting From Your Knees

*DVDs:*

Animal Day: Pressure Testing the Martial Arts

Animal Day Part Two: The Fights

Three Second Fighter: The Sniper Option

Throws and Takedowns Vols. 1- 6

Real Punching Vols. 1-3

The Fence

*Ground Fighting Series*

Vol 1 Pins: The Bedrock

Vol 2 The Escapes

Vol 3 Chokes and Strangles

Vol 4 Arm Bars and Joint Locks

Vol 5 Fighting From Your Back

Vol 6 Fighting From Your Knees

Advanced Ground Fighting Vols. 1-3

Pavement Arena Part 1

Pavement Arena Part 2: The Protection Pyramid

Pavement Arena Part 3: Grappling. The Last Resort

Pavement Arena Part 4: Fit To Fight

For more details visit www.geoffthompson.com

For a free colour brochure of Geoff Thompson products ring/fax 02476 431100 or write to Geoff Thompson @ PO Box 307 Coventry, West Midlands CV3 2YP.

Thank you very much to Rachael Osborne for her patience and guidance in editing this book. Thank you to Kerry Thompson for the first edit.

Dedicated to the memory of my lovely friend James Gillies who died in 1998 after a long and brave battle with cancer. You remain a great inspiration to me James, I love you. God bless.

A little boy can be paralysed with fear
when he is told there is a bogie man under
his bed who is going to take him away. When
his father turns on the light and shows him
there is no bogie man, he is freed from
fear. The fear in the mind of the boy was as
real as if there was a bogie man there. He was
healed of a false thought in his mind.
The thing he feared did not exist.
Likewise, most of your fears have no reality.
They are merely a conglomeration of sinister
shadows, and shadows have no reality.

Dr Joseph Murphy
*The Power of Your Subconscious Mind*

LET'S TURN ON THE LIGHTS!

# Contents

# Introduction

Welcome to *Stress Buster*. My sole intention with this book is to offer solace to those of you out there who may be suffering the consequences of fear and stress. It is not a motivational book – though it does motivate in places – neither is it meant to be. Rather it is a book for the seriously stressed. I hope to offer solace in big chunks by explaining the mechanics of fear and why the feeling of wanting to run away from confrontational moments in life is both expected and natural. We all feel fear; it's how we deal with it that determines where our lives might lead. My intention is to put a name to some of the problems our species face, because to name something gives us a certain amount of power over it.

Most people misread, and therefore mismanage, fear. Subsequently, they live a metaphoric prison existence in a comfort cell under the wardenship of ignorance and surrounded by bars of fear.

Man was not fashioned to kill man and yet we are living in a world where war, our greatest expression of violence, is not only frequent but also seen as normal. Recent surveys carried out on human warfare have demonstrated not only man's antipathy toward self-destruction but also his predilection to run from conflict as opposed to standing and fighting.

It is evident that when our survival is threatened or we feel that it is, our impulse to turn and run is far stronger than it is to stand and fight. So much so that if the flight option is negated, the greater majority of us would rather risk death than kill another of the same species. Either obliviously or deliberately, we become conscientious objectors at the point of pulling the trigger. The survey intimated that the greater majority of soldiers fired their bullets into the ground, high into the air or they did not shoot at all.

This is what I call the Minority Rule; the minority of soldiers in major human conflicts are responsible for the majority of the killings. In the Second World War for instance, it was reported that only 15–20 per cent of combat infantry were willing to fire their rifles.[1]

I'm sure we all agree that an aversion to killing and the urge to escape threat is desirable and essential to our survival, but the Minority Rule does have some major shortfalls in contemporary society. Problems start to arise when our socially under-evolved mid-brain (the part of the brain that deals with fight or flight) fails to distinguish between real threat and that which is imagined. The mid-brain perceives all threat as physical and therefore, in most confrontational situations (real or imagined), we are apt to freeze or feel the natural urge to run away. To our survival mechanism every stressor is a war, often in microcosm, but a war nevertheless. And the majority of us, when faced with conflict of any kind, are likely to become conscientious objectors at the onset of fear. What this important fact tells us is that the majority of people do not want to, and most often will not, enter into what they perceive as a threatening conflict.

I believe our natural instinct to withdraw is stronger than any other emotion we might experience; certainly it is stronger than the willpower of the greater majority. And it is only a concrete and well-disciplined will that might allow us to override our instincts when flight is neither an answer or an option. Our ignorance in matters relating to fear is also, in my view, responsible for the majority of world conflict. If we knew more about ourselves – and therefore our fellow man – we would have less reason to fear him and more reason to love and forgive him.

This would encourage a greater propensity toward leniency and compassion in affairs that might need a change of dynamics rather than a charge of dynamite. As it is, we seem prepared to fight over just about any issue that is sponsored by ignorance and fear. We constantly fight over boundaries, whether they are ideological (personal beliefs), environmental (the environment), psychological (ego), theological (religious) or geographical (land). I'm ashamed to say that we even kill in the name of The Deity that said we should forgive not 7 times but 47 times 7.

We also have a paradox at play in this capricious era. If we listen to our oldest instincts and flee from potential danger we feel, or are often made to feel, like cowards and shunned by our peers. However, if we should find ourselves cornered and engage in a physical fight we become criminals and thugs and are incarcerated. It seems hypocrisy in our society knows no bounds.

The instinct to run as opposed to fight, as stated earlier, is deeply gene-embedded and dates back to mammalian ancestry. Our impulses in that dangerous era were sharply honed to survival at any cost; this usually meant fleeing from wild, threatening animals that were too big or dangerous to stand up to and fight.

Unfortunately, or fortunately depending upon your viewpoint, these instincts are still with us, though they have not evolved to meet the contemporary stressor. The mid-brain cannot discern between the sabre-toothed tiger and any of its modern day equivalents; marital disputes, talking in public, business deadlines, confrontation with the boss, exams, personal challenges or traffic jams.

Running or fighting for your life is all well and good but what if that stressor is imagined, symbolic or vague and there is nothing to run away from or fight? We spend our entire lives fleeing from metaphoric tigers or fighting projectional duels on displaced battlefields. Alternatively, we might find ourselves frozen by an ill-defined stressor that dulls the aptitude with confusion, tension, anxiety, withdrawal and inactivity.

In short, many people fail to live their dreams because of fear; every stressor becomes a physical threat that our chemical and electrical messengers heed us to flee from. This equates to non-achievement and a non-productive existence. The ambiguous fear signals create a prison for our entrepreneurial selves and stop us from evolving.

The contemporary stressor cannot be fought or escaped on a physical plain. The challenge therefore must be met by other means. We need a better understanding of the unconscious workings of the human body. We must nurture the development of will. And we should employ coping mechanisms to help us avoid, escape or manage the physical, psychological and spiritual aspects of fear. Only then will inappropriate and antiquated instinct effectively evolve.

Over the next couple of generations we have to help our survival instincts in this quest so that we might realise our full potential as a species, grow in consciousness and metamorphose into more spiritual beings. This might sound ideological, it might even sound corny, but I believe that we can be so much more than we are right now. Life is so (potentially) exciting, there is so much that we can be, do and enjoy but we are blocked by our own fears. In many ways our greatest underlying fear is our own potential, deep down we know that we are princes but the very thought frightens us into staying paupers. We need to grow in consciousness, and therefore in spirituality, we need more knowledge and this cannot be achieved whilst our fear impedes us. By overcoming our own fears we can release and realise our greatest potential.

A friend told me about an incident that really disturbed him. He was disgusted by the actions of several 'cowardly' men in a virtual reality game he visited in London. The game involved being locked into a small room and exposed to a pretend war scenario. The men in question, with their girlfriends and wives, eagerly anticipated the fun when suddenly the doors crashed open and a group of soldiers burst in firing automatic weapons (part of the game). Three of the men ran for the door in an attack of panic. One even elbowed his girlfriend in the face to escape. Unconsciously they believed the danger to be real and centuries of instinct went into action. They fled for their lives.

I explained to my friend that these men were not cowards, neither should they be judged for or by their actions, they did nothing more than listen to natural instinct. As far as their survival mechanism was concerned they did exactly the right thing. And if you think that my friend was disgusted, imagine how badly these men must have felt about themselves. Because of self-ignorance they will probably brand *themselves* cowards and carry the subsequent guilt to their graves.

It takes great understanding, will-power and specific training to override natural instinct. If the training is aimed at overcoming intangible threats then the concept is not only sound but also imperative. If however the training is aimed at overcoming our natural disinclination to kill then the concept has serious drawbacks that need to be addressed.

In the Vietnam War American soldiers were taught, via specific desensitisation and dehumanisation techniques, to override their natural disinclination to kill, and the Minority

Rule was reversed. The majority (90 per cent) of the American soldiers in Vietnam were responsible for the majority of the killings.[2]

## The Cortisol Connection

Our ancestral instinct is badly outdated and gone crazy in a society exposed to more neurological stressors than ever before. The fight or flight instinct operates via the senses and triggers adrenalin (and other stress hormones such as cortisol) when it senses imminent danger. In theory this is fine; it prepares us for life and death battles with aggressors. In actuality it has major drawbacks because our senses are constantly being attacked by stimuli that might be aggressive but most often are not. Even the loud horn of a car can trigger fight or flight, releasing a cocktail of stress hormones in anticipation of an affray that never materialises.

Moving jobs, moving house, changing partners, marital conflict or stress at work may cause enough concern to fool the brain into thinking they are in fact sabre-toothed tigers. This triggers the release of adrenalin that is not used by the body because there is no fight or flight. Due to this we are left aroused and with the very corrosive effect of cortisol in our bodies.

Cortisol is very corrosive. It attacks the smooth internal muscles (heart, lungs, intestines) and has been linked with many debilitating illnesses; it has been strongly linked with Alzheimer's disease because of the part it plays in destroying brain cells. Hence our survival structure is killing us from the inside out.

Our bodies, perhaps sensing this danger, try to expel the residue or waste by displacing it, usually via a physical act; perhaps sport or our work (if the work is physical), but more often via inappropriate actions like road rage, marital disputes, temper tantrums, irrational behaviour and very often violence.

It doesn't take a degree in psychology to realise that stress hormones left in the body leave the recipient in an aroused state with displacement being the usual method of release. Usually displacement occurs unconsciously, in the home, in the car, at the pub. And the more vague stressors we engage, the more Rogue Stress Hormones we collect until arousal reaches bursting point. This eventually creates a pressure cooker effect; arousal is so high the recipient explodes in an uncontrolled manner at the slightest provocation.

The Rogue Hormone

Jim was a very successful bookmaker. His job held no real physical threat, though it could be confrontational, especially if a customer hit a losing streak. Jim's main stress came from the threat of losing money; if the punters won their bets he lost money. His brain registered this trepidation as a sabre-toothed tiger several times a day and he would get massive adrenalin injections into his body that found no physical release.

His release came at the end of each day; often on his girlfriend and family. Arriving home after a stressful day he'd spend his evening in procrastination, arguing with the people he loved most. Jim was one of the most violently aggressive men I have ever met. He was like a time bomb constantly waiting to go off. He never held a relationship down for very long because his violent outbursts became intolerable for any potential suitor.

This mild-mannered man with a shy smile would become a demon after a day of stress.

You might think that after years of failed relationships Jim might have figured it out. Unfortunately not. He assured me that his rages were the fault of his girlfriend, his mother, his father, the driver who cut him up on the road, the chap in the pub who spilled his beer. He was one of the many who never learned because he could not accept responsibility.

Jim's violent outbursts overflowed into physical abuse and he physically attacked many of the women he dated. Jim is a lovely looking man, very fit and usually very gentle but when the stress is high he strikes out with violence.

He has even taken counselling (under advisement), which is good, though privately he still insists on projecting the blame on to anyone other than himself.

I am aware of course that this man may have a bigger, more deep-seated problem that needs to be addressed, but fundamentally his problem is one of displacement and denial.

Unlike another gentleman who came to train with me at my karate school. I explained the concept of adrenal overload and displacement to the class one lesson. He got it in one. He said it was a revelation. He approached me the next week. 'I now understand' he told me, 'why I have been such a pig to my wife for the last three years!'

Apparently he'd been under a lot of stress at work and inadvertently took it home with him. He became very aggressive, irrational and snappy with his lady to the point that it was ruining their marriage. As soon as he understood his problem he went straight home to his wife with flowers and chocolates and apologised for his mistreatment. He said the information probably saved his marriage.

When you find yourself looking for a fight with others and blaming them it creates more problems that it solves. It does get the stress out of you but, when you argue and fight, it also triggers more stress. If you displace your stress on your wife for instance, she'll understandably be upset. She might not speak to you for a few days. Certainly there will be tension in the home and in the top ten of most stressful events, marital discord rates right up there with the best of them.

Similarly, someone who displaces their stress in road rage will, potentially, create a lot more stress if the other driver argues or fights back or if there is police involvement.

Other people suppress or repress the build-up of stress rather than release it unfairly on to others, and whilst this may be magnanimous, it certainly is not healthy. It does little more than drive the stress underground, where it ferments and builds in intensity. In the long-term this is highly detrimental to health. It can promote mild to serious, even fatal, illness.

All this and more will be explored throughout this book. It is my sincere hope that you will find solace, health and personal power in this information. Don't allow fear and ignorance to stop you from loving your life.

# Chapter One
# **Understanding the Enemy**

Understanding the enemy is predominantly what this book is all about. They say that knowledge is power: in this case it certainly is.

We need, at the very least, a basic understanding of our own bodies if we are going to get through this life in one piece. Unfortunately people seem to know more about the engines in their cars than they do the internal workings of their own bodies. Most of us go through a whole lifetime without ever understanding ourselves, or others for that matter. The good thing about understanding yourself is that, once you do, you automatically have a very good understanding of others because biologically we are all made of the same stuff.

Understanding myself had a profound influence on the way I handled potentially violent situations in my capacity as a nightclub doorman. As a young bouncer I didn't know the first thing about myself. What I knew didn't extend far beyond what I saw in the shaving mirror every morning. The real me, the one hiding on the inside, was almost a complete stranger.

Before the doors – and whenever a violent situation reared its ugly head – my instinct was always to run away from confrontation. With the benefit of hindsight I understand this to be a natural and expected feeling. Without retrospect I felt like a coward. I felt completely alone, the only one in the world who felt this scared. My ignorance created a lot of self-doubt. I equated wanting to run away with weakness. As a beginner I allowed these very strong emotions to overwhelm me and I ran away from most of life's confrontational moments. I was the running man! And each time I ran I made it harder for myself to make a stand the next time fear came calling. With a history of defeat behind me failure became my norm.

To overcome this lack I set about confronting my fears. I developed my will until it was strong enough to override the inclination to leg it every time I sensed fear. However, I still struggled with the discomfort of adrenalin and subsequently, as a fledgling doorman, I would attack my antagonists as soon as I could, usually too soon, just to get it over and done with. Customers who just wanted to vent a bit of aggression in my direction got a punch in the eye (or worse) for their troubles. I became feared very quickly, and at the time I thought this was a good thing. Now I can see how awful and also how stupid I was to think that people fearing me led to people respecting me. In a reciprocal world such as ours, fear attracts nothing but more fear and its ugly handmaiden violence. Basically, every time I felt fear I hit someone. I was the proverbial caveman, with an ugly club as my means of communication. Because of this I acquired a reputation as a hair trigger, a man who hit first and asked questions later.

As I became more familiar with adrenalin I developed a profound understanding of its mechanics. I learned how to handle anticipation for longer and longer periods. Sometimes, in the case of threats of reprisal, for months at a time.

I also realised, from talking to the other doormen, that we all feel the same, to varying degrees, some just hide it better than others. So I no longer associated the release of adrenalin and the subsequent feelings with cowardice, or even with fear. It was simply a biological preparation for what my brain thought was a life or death battle with the elements. It was natural, as natural as wanting to go to the bathroom, or feeling hungry or thirsty.

I sowed the seed of self-knowledge and reaped confidence and understanding from its wisdom. As a consequence I found myself hitting less people and applying the use of verbal communication as opposed to the use of force – which a lot of people in Coventry were very happy about. I also started to experiment with the fear syndrome. I exposed myself to varying kinds of stress and then practised different coping strategies, some I had read about and others I made up as I went along.

## The Fear Pyramid

I developed the Fear Pyramid as a means to overcoming fear and building a strong will.

The Fear Pyramid can be a very private thing. I know that a lot of people would not wish to share their more private fears with others. This reticence is understandable and, unless you want to enlist the help of others in overcoming fears, you don't need to publicly divulge your more private apprehensions. What I'm saying is you don't need to take out an advertisement in the local rag announcing your deeper thoughts with the populace. I certainly didn't, though I have to say it does lessen the burden if you have someone trustworthy to share the load. A problem shared and all that.

What is imperative is self-honesty; you need to admit your fears, if only to yourself. Don't fob yourself off, as I once did, with defence mechanisms (see later chapter) like, 'I'm not scared of it (what ever 'it' may be), I just don't want to do it', and other such nonsense.

This is the first and most important step; you can go no further until this is complete. Even an alcoholic cannot begin treatment until he first admits that he is an alcoholic.

These are the four preparatory steps:

1. Admit your fears, even if it is only to yourself. If this first step is not in place you cannot realistically expect to go any further.

2. Make a list of all your fears.

3. Draw a pyramid with as many, or as few, steps up to the pinnacle as you have fears.

4. Fill each of those steps with one of your listed fears starting at the bottom of the pyramid with your least fear and finishing at the top step with your greatest fear.

# fred's fear Pyramid

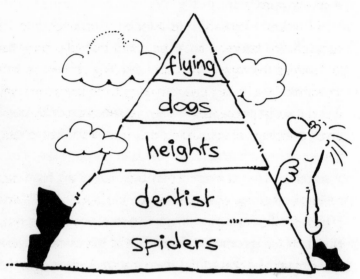

The common factor with all fears is that confronting them will cause physiological fight or flight, the release of adrenaline into the body; it is our perception of danger, even if that supposed danger is only symbolic, that causes anticipation and adrenal release.

For greater detail on the Fear Pyramid I'd recommend that you read my book, *Fear: The Friend of Exceptional People*, where the subject is dealt with more comprehensively.

When I was a self-defence instructor I very often come across people who told me they felt like cowards because they had previously run away from confrontations. One man said, 'I've been training for twenty years and yet when the fight kicked off I just ran away. I felt so scared. I feel like such a coward.'

He wasn't a coward. He listened to instinct, and he survived. His failure, if it can be called that, was only that he misread the signs. What his reasoning process saw as 'cowardice' was in fact ego reminding him that to run away was not socially acceptable. The punishment for this social error is feelings of cowardice, low self-worth, regret and guilt.

Another friend, a very successful businessman, had been offered an exciting opportunity to live and work in the United States, but was scared to make the move. 'I've been working all my life for this opportunity,' he told me sincerely, 'and when it's finally offered to me on a plate I haven't got the guts to go for it.'

He too felt like a coward and that he was letting everyone down. He was not a coward, he misread the signs, that's all. The feelings he experienced were natural anticipation, which he allowed to grow into fully-fledged fear with horns on. Anyone would feel a little nervous about such a big decision, even if it were planned for.

When I explained my thoughts on the matter he dropped the 'I'm weak, I'm such a coward' routine and brought his fattened apprehension to heel. He stood his fear in front of him and shone a little light on it, and low and behold the beggar fell apart like a cheap suit and disappeared never to be seen again. Then he got on with the job of emigrating and extending his success to a bigger circus.

You too can master your own emotions by understanding yourself and your bodily reactions to apprehension. It's OK to be scared, we all are, it is what you do with that fear that makes your life either a heaven or a hell.

# Chapter Two
# Understanding the Other
# – It's Not Personal!

I spent some time in America teaching at a convention with Chuck Norris, Rigan Machodo and a guy called Benny 'The Jet' Urquediz. All legendary martial art stars. I was sitting talking with Benny one afternoon when a little lad came running up to him, excited. He had just confronted his fears and entered a very hard karate contest. Benny stopped our conversation and said to the boy, 'How did you do?' The little lad smiled and said, 'I won.' Benny said, 'Did you do what I said?' 'Yes,' he replied, full of smiles, 'I didn't take any of it personally.'

One of the great things about learning to understand yourself is that it automatically, though often inadvertently, teaches you a hell of a lot about other people. Once we understand the mechanics of our own body and mind it helps us better understand the bodies and minds of those around us. Biologically we are all made of the same stuff! I can't tell you what a difference this has made to me. Now that I know myself and others I no longer take it all so personally.

## Road Rage

For instance, my current understanding of stress (and displacement) allows me to better understand the irate driver who is trying to vent his anger on me over some minor traffic incident. I now understand what's going on in his mind (probably more so that he understands himself). I can clearly see that I am little more than a manifestation of some pending dilemma that he might have. This is not about him and me, rather it is about him and his bullying boss or perhaps him and his over-dominant wife. In fact, I might be a manifestation of all that is wrong with his life. One thing I have learned and one thing I know is this: it's not personal! Unless, as Jean Luc Picard says, we make it so. This information allows me to be more tolerant with those who are perhaps trying my patience. I can let it go and just walk away because I understand that it's more to do with his stress than it is to do with me. It is not personal – most of the time. In the case of road rage the other person probably can't even see me through the windscreen of their car, I'm just some faceless person who has activated his Vesuvius (it's a volcano), I am possibly the final straw on the back of a very stressed and angry camel. Because I understand this I don't take it personally, how can I? The guy needs my sympathy more than he needs my fist in his face. Because it's not personal, and I understand why this red-faced, angry person is ranting and raving at me from his vehicle, I don't take it personally. I refuse to. I can instantly let it go and drive off.

Next time the guy in front fails to signal, or cuts you up, or drives dangerously, sit and think for a second. Look at the consequences of getting out of your vehicle and entering into an affray (with goodness knows who), he could be a mass murderer or a Mafia boss for all you know. Then, instead of joining in and becoming a part of the rage, take a look in an honest mirror. Ask yourself a question; 'Have I never made a similar mistake?'

Let me ask you this (and be honest), do you think for one single solitary moment that giving the other driver a piece of your mind is going to make the slightest bit of positive difference to the way he drives his car? I doubt it. What it will do is perhaps trigger his trapped aggression and create a physical contention that might change the course of both your lives. There is a massive responsibility that comes with impulsive and aggressive behaviour. I know loads of my mates are doing time, and a couple are dead because they acted before thinking of the end result. People die in road rage incidents you know.

I used to get wound up and in the car, I was Road Rage Man. I was forever red-in-the-head about bad drivers who didn't use the road quite to my liking. Then one day I caught a glimpse of myself in an honest mirror. I remember thinking, 'Who is this ranting maniac? This bully?' And that's what I was, a bully, there was no other word for it. I was ashamed of myself. If any other driver made a mistake (ironically, mistakes that *I* had made a million times before) I'd be shaking my fist and using words that started with 'F' and 'B' to admonish them. And, if needs be, I was prepared to get out of the car and have a bit on the tarmac with them. It was then I realised the truth. I was weak! It's true. That's what I was; a very weak person who couldn't control himself. Not just that, I was a puppet. Controlled by anyone who fancied a pull at my rather sensitive strings. If someone gave me the finger in the car, or beeped their horn a little too loud, or cut in front of me, or even nodding-dogged their head when I cut in front of them, I'd think nothing of giving chase. Sometimes for miles. Other times I'd give them the finger right back, followed by the usual warning of what I'd do if they ever dared cross me. Pushed, I might even get out of the car myself and give theirs an angry boot in the side door. And we're a civilised society? I'm embarrassed to say I was one of the many being led around on an ego lead. Risking all for nothing.

Now, with my ego starving to death in a self-imposed prison of self-control, I don't fight over a space on the slip road. I don't curse or judge when other drivers run wild at the mouth and I certainly don't bite when an ego spews its aggression from a very fast car. It's not personal. I just smile to myself, give Sarah Cox a bit more volume on Radio One and contemplate better ways to spend my energy.

So drive on, there can be no argument or contention if you're not there to argue or contend with.

Road rage is big news in the 1990s and the psychologists are making a big issue about the causes. They talk about personal space, invasion of territory, even poor potty training as a child gets its fair share of blame. And maybe there's a bit of truth in all of it, but I believe the main problem is plain and simple. Displacement. We've even seen people killed in road rage incidents. It's a growing problem that needs addressing.

Probably the majority of all confrontational situations can be avoided if we don't take it all so personally. Of the minority that can't be avoided, most can be handled without violence (verbal or physical) if we have know-how.

Why is all of this so relevant? Because when we take it all personally it makes us anxious and anxiety triggers the release of stress hormones, then the whole downward spiral begins. Physiological fight or flight is a physical syndrome that needs a physical release. If there is no direct or tangible exit for the unused adrenalin, a surrogate one will, usually unconsciously, be found.

Many people in stressful occupations take their stress home to their spouses who become the manifestation of their aggression. This, I believe, is one of the main causes of divorce and marriage breakdown in occupations like security, the police, politics and the stock exchange. Those living or working in a very stressful environment tend to experience multiple releases of unutilised adrenalin throughout a single day. This saturates the system with hormones looking for a fight. If there isn't a fight immediately available eventually they will find one of their own making. The slightest incident triggers them and some poor soul gets the whole lot.

I experienced this first hand in my years working as a nightclub doorman in Coventry. For weeks on end I would get release after release of adrenalin for fights that I thought might happen but that never did. Because there was no physical (or what psychologists call 'behavioural') release I'd be left highly aroused and vulnerable to inadvertent triggers. One of the many occasions that my aggression found an accidental outlet was when my ex-wife triggered a two-month build up of stress.

I had been receiving threats of violence via the phone and the grapevine after a fight with a local gang. After two months of this I was so highly strung that, one afternoon, I jumped over a neighbour's hedge when a passing car backfired and on another occasion I attacked a cat that sprang from an entry on my way home from the club. I've never been so embarrassed in my life.

I didn't know what was going on inside me at the time. I only knew I was a hair trigger and very uneasy – even dangerous – to be around. My (former) wife told me so, only in richer terms. It wasn't me, I claimed. It was her, anyone could see that. It was her fault for being such a nag! Within seconds of telling her this (I think it was the word 'nag' that did it) I was wearing my dinner and very nice it looked too. The disagreement that became an argument suddenly became a raging battle. Before I knew it I'd made matchsticks of the bedroom furniture (I knew my martial arts training would come in handy at some point), and she'd made an exit for her mother's.

My fit of displaced aggression was completely out of proportion with the triggering stimuli (the argument). It frightened my ex half to death. She was very upset. 'You need to see a ******* head doctor,' she said as the door slammed behind her. Due to the fact that I didn't understand about displacement, I was half inclined to agree with her. The only solace I could take at the time was the fact that many of my friends (fellow doormen) were experiencing similar problems and we all agreed on one point, that it wasn't us – it was them. Although we didn't understand the reasoning behind our violence we felt it helped to know that that we were not alone. Another thing I didn't realise at the time, and what I have since learned, was that these accidental triggers were not the cause of our problems. They were not to blame; rather they were simply the catalysts, the physical manifestations of many previously unresolved conflicts.

The accidental release is not good. Whilst it does release trapped adrenalin it is not controlled and by its very nature it courts and perpetuates further stress. The amount of stress I got from my ex after smashing up her bedroom was equal or worse than the stress I started out with.

Every argument ended with two weeks of microwave dinners, takeaways and a cold back in bed.

I know some of you may demonstrate more self-control than I did – and you are to be lauded for that – thinking this is the answer. It's not, I'm afraid. Those who stoically plug their stress with tufts of self-control are no better off unfortunately. Admirable as this might seem it is not the solution, far from it. Holding it all in subjects the internal organs to a deadly cocktail of stress hormones, specifically cortisol, that are a toxic bath for the smooth internal muscle tissue.

The toxic bath

As previously stated, stress hormones stimulate and arouse us for a physical response. If a physical response is not necessary and the stress hormones do not find their way out, they stay in the body. These are what I call Rogue Hormones and they are constantly in search of a tangible release (a fight or flight). When not released, and for the time that they stay in your body, they are detrimental to health in ways that we will explore later.[3]

So holding it all in is no better than actually letting it all out in an uncontrolled manner because of the internal devastation it creates.

## A Solution

One solution, and it's been my salvation, is what I call the Safe Surrogate Release (SSR) that clears the toxins from your system without creating further stress. A safe release for the Rogue Hormones.

The SSR is a physical (or molar) action that acts as a surrogate release for the hormones that are trapped in your body. This might be a vigorous game of tennis, a squash match, football, rugby, dancing or running. Basically anything that gets up a bit of a sweat will be a good release for the trapped hormones. They're running round looking for fight or flight and when you hit the tennis ball or dance the waltz they think, 'this is it, let's get it on!' and go to work, releasing themselves in a physical action.

Basically, and very crudely, it's the same as going to the toilet to get rid of the day's physical waste. With the SSR we are getting rid of the psychological and physiological waste.

You imagine eating normally and not getting rid of the waste by going to the toilet. You'd be bursting at the seams by the end of the week. Not only would it start forcing its way out (very messy), it'd also be impossible to function because poisons would seep into your system. It's similar with stress. We are collecting stress hormones that are not being used; this creates a natural waste that is not excreted. It's no wonder we become uncomfortable and irritable after a day of business deadlines, or an hour stuck in traffic. By the end of the day, week, month or even year we will be bursting at the seams.

Understanding the self is understanding our capacity to store negative stress and inadvertently displace it on to others. Understanding ourselves automatically lends itself to understanding others because we are fundamentally the same. If we accidentally take our stress out on others they are as likely to do the same right back.

We will look at the SSR and how to use it in more detail later in the book.

## Chapter Three
# The Inverted U Hypothesis

I know this might sound a bit convoluted, it certainly did to me the first time I heard it, but it's not really, it's very simple (honestly). The Inverted U Hypothesis is basically just an upside down U that allows us to measure when stress is good for us – because sometimes it is – and at what point it becomes bad.

### Inverted U Hypothesis

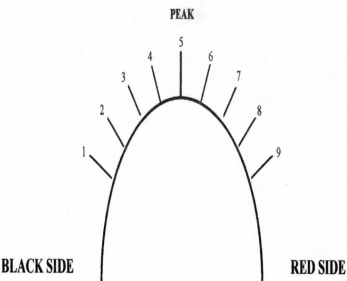

Looking at the diagram, everything to the left-hand side of the U can be good for us, it gives us drive, energy and it helps us to achieve. We need a degree of stress in our lives for this reason. At number three and four, just left of the peak, we are probably at our most productive. There is enough stress to give us drive but not so much that we can't cope. When we hit number five on the peak of the U, we are usually very productive but also very vulnerable because there is a constant danger of toppling over the edge. At number five (the peak) we are very precariously balanced indeed and whilst we might be able to just cope we are very vulnerable to overload should one or more new stressors suddenly appear on the scene. Similarly to just balancing financially in the bank, you're not in debt, but you're not flush either. You cope fine with this balance until one, two or three bills unexpectedly drop through the letterbox and take you into overdraft. All of a sudden you're in the red.

Stressors, like pound notes, are the very same. Real problems start to occur on the inverted U when, already on the peak and under pressure, Bang! Unexpected stressors suddenly appear and we topple over the edge. This lands us on the right-hand side (number 6 and above) where stress becomes bad for us. One minute we are balancing nicely in the black, the next we are sinking quickly into the red.

These added stressors don't need to be huge to over balance you. It could be something as simple as a minor dispute with a neighbour, perhaps the tax bill arrives, maybe you're given extra responsibility at work, it could be anything.

Suddenly you have more on your cart than the wheels can take.

If you were working at the positive side of the inverted U (numbers 2, 3 or 4) these extra stressors, though still perhaps unwanted, would be quite manageable. But because you're at the peak and already working to your limit they knock you right over the edge and you struggle to cope.

If allowed, these new stressors will eat up all your energy and you'll find yourself on the downward spiral. Once on this slippery slope we hit what is known as stress degeneration; our tolerance levels drop and we get stressed about things that wouldn't normally bother us at all. Things that, on the left of the U, we'd cope easily with suddenly penetrate our defences and make their mark. Once under this kind of pressure, and with little or no defence, we start to see (or even create) problems that are not, or were not actually there. At the peak we can cope, even though it may be a struggle, but at numbers six and above we falter, even fall. We are, as they say in banking terms, overdrawn.

The downward spiral

The longer we find ourselves over the edge of the inverted U the more vulnerable we become to new stressors because we are expending energy that we don't actually have, that we have borrowed from a reserve tank. The more energy we expend, the weaker we become and thus the more we expose ourselves to further stressors that will, in their own turn pull us down further still.

Being over the edge of the inverted U for long periods of time can be very detrimental to health. It can attack and severely weaken the nervous and immune system. So we need to get back on to the left-hand side of the U again, and quickly.

## Borrowing Energy

I've spent a lot of time in the red (over the edge of the U) and it was only the fact that I knew I was at risk, and what I had to do to get back in balance again, that saved my bacon. Even then it was a real struggle, at times I thought I might not make it. I have several friends that didn't.

When we're in the red for too long and constantly borrowing energy to survive, we have a problem. If you are already overdrawn where do you borrow from? In bank terms you might take out a loan that has to be repaid, or extend your overdraft. In bodily terms we borrow from ourselves, that is, we start to feed off surplus energy stored in the body. The stress response (especially once in the red) is a turbo drive that uses up tremendous amounts of fuel. When there isn't enough immediate fuel (taken from what we have eaten) it starts to draw stored energy from bodyweight. It will even use protein (muscle) as energy if body fat is too low. Once protein levels become dangerously low we also start to feed off nervous energy. This is where we are at our most vulnerable and a physical or nervous breakdown can easily occur.

I had several friends around the country who allowed themselves to get so far over the edge and into energy debt with the nervous system that their constitutions collapsed and they committed suicide. The nervous system will reluctantly borrow your emergency fuel but, I have to say, it is an unsympathetic lender that will bankrupt you without hesitation should you not honour the debt.

For those training fanatics out there (of which I have been one) energy debt is almost permanently on the agenda and there is a constant and real danger of going over the top. Training in moderation is a great stress buster. Taken to extremes the training is so hard it becomes a stressor in itself. I have personally witnessed this many times with friends, colleagues and myself.

On one occasion, training for my second Dan black belt in Shotokan Karate, I was hitting the gym three times a day, working a full-time job and managing a family, all at the same time. I lost a stone in weight without even realising and became (not for the first time) clinically depressed. So much so that my doctor tried to put me on antidepressants. This was probably the lowest point of my life. I was so stressed and depressed (the two seem to go hand in hand) that I felt there was nothing to live for. The ring of the phone would set my nerves a-rattling, sleep escaped me at night, though I kept falling asleep in the day, and even the smallest of decisions became major stressors to me. I felt so weak and so low that I didn't want to do anything at all. Everything in my life felt confrontational so I tried as hard as I could to avoid people and lock myself away from what I believed was a cruel world. On that particular occasion it was the fight of my life to get out of the red and into the black.

Stress and Depression - the two seem to go hand in hand.

## Making Positive Decisions

Getting back into the black is less about taking antidepressants (although at times this can be a crutch) and more about taking the stressor out of your life by making positive decisions. These decisions have to be made quickly whilst the energy levels allow. The longer you have to cope in the red the more your energy levels deplete and therefore the less strength you have to face and make those vital decisions.

The moment you realise you're over the edge of the U is the very moment you should start to make decisions to lighten the load. These will be strong decisions. If you are carrying three stressors too many then three stressors have to go to get you back into the black.

Making decisions with the hypothetical example I gave earlier might mean knocking on the neighbour's door and mending the rift, apologise if it's your fault, agree to disagree if fault can not be found. Ring up the tax people and explain your dilemma, ask for a little more time to pay your bill or even arrange to send them three post-dated cheques that will cover the bill over a three or four monthly period. Delegate some of the load at work on to others, or simply approach your boss and ask them for a little help. What I have found in situations like this is: the buck stops with you. If you don't make the decisions they won't get made. And we can spend as long as we like procrastinating about how bad the world is and 'why me?' and blaming others but it won't make the slightest difference. Rather the opposite in fact. You'll be using up energy moaning and worrying which will increase your debt rather than lessen it. Probably my greatest life lesson so far: it's down to us! We are the creators (or certainly co-creators with God); we have the ability to create. This means we can have anything we want, and do anything we want! But there is a responsibility that comes with this knowledge. Once we accept charge we can no longer blame anyone else when things go wrong. Also, we have to be very careful and respectful of this great power because if we misuse it we might create bad things. Whatever you sow, so shall you reap (as the saying goes). It's not mystical, it's not some conditional God punishing you for your sins, it's just basic science, cause and effect, action and consequence. When you pick up one end of the stick, you also pick up the other.

Often when things are not going too well you feel as though your back is against the wall, but it never is. There's always a way out, you just have to search for it. Once you find the solution and act upon it you are on your way 'back to black.'

I remember an occasion in my early twenties. Two of my friends were thinking about starting their own company and, due to my qualifications in their specific area, they asked me to front the company. At first I was very flattered, the thought of heading a company was nice, even though it was not really practical at the time. Beneath the flattered front I knew I was still far too inexperienced in my field to run this company, but, for all the wrong reasons, I felt that I should give it a go.

For the next month my mind was filled with nothing else. I looked deeply into the premise of the company, and my ability to run it. The more I looked the more I realised I was out of my depth. It wasn't that I was scared to take on the job, it was just that at that time I was grossly and obviously under-qualified and under-experienced. But I felt it had already gone too far to back out.

My friends were really excited about the business and I didn't want to let them down. To make up for my inexperience I started to study the company subject matter more and more, thinking that I might be able to cram years of experience into several weeks.

There wasn't a minute of the day that I wasn't thinking about, practising or researching for this new company, as well as trying to fit in a full-time job and look after my family. At the same time I was using energy up at a rate of knots with confusion.

Expending lots of energy on a business idea is great when you have focus and inspiration because focus and inspiration give you energy, they actually recharge you. But when you have no focus and no inspiration because you know you are hacking away in the wrong jungle, all you are doing is emptying the bank and putting nothing back in.

In a very short time I was well and truly over the edge of the inverted U. Add to this the fact that the stress, worry, confusion (should I be doing this or should I stop, is it right or wrong?) and overwork killed my appetite. Subsequently I hardly ate a thing, and what I did eat didn't nearly cover the amount of fuel I was using to think and to study. I was borrowing hand over fist from the nervous system and my energy debt was starting to cause depression. At the time I didn't have a clue why I felt so weak and down, the world suddenly looked very dark to me. I didn't know about the inverted U, borrowing energy or energy debt. I knew nothing, only that I was feeling more depressed by the day.

My whole world became dark and I lost all interest in everything. I would burst out crying for the slightest thing and then feel ashamed afterwards because 'men don't do that!' My shame became another stressor that demanded more energy. When I went to bed at night the feelings of depression loomed over me vulture-like, foreboding hung in my chest like a lead weight. It haunted my sleep, and when I awoke from a fitful night it was there waiting for me. My biggest mistake was allowing depression to bully me. My depression became a stressor itself, which triggered more stress hormones, used more energy creating more debt and, subsequently, more depression. I was on the downward spiral and slipping fast.

In the end it was only a strong decision on my part that saved the day. I told my friends that, whilst I was very flattered, the company was not for me. I thought the news might really upset them and in retrospect that thought had been my greatest worry. I didn't want to let them down. But they weren't let down. In fact quite the opposite, they didn't seem that bothered. And even if they were let down, so what? The decisions you make in life sometimes have to be selfish. How can you put your heart into something if your heart is not in it? How can you help others without first helping yourself? How can you save a drowning man if you yourself are drowning? First you have to lead yourself then you can lead others. It's hard to lead a cavalry if you think you look silly sitting on a horse.

I can see now my greatest enemies in this scenario, and what took me into energy debt. 1) Over-consideration for what others would think of me if I said no (ego). Which in turn led to over thinking and 2) poor decision-making. Which leads to bouts of prolonged stress. 3) I set myself an impossible task (trying to cram years of experience into a matter of weeks).

I can see now that I allowed myself to be drawn into a position that I knew I wasn't ready for, because I lacked the maturity and strength to say 'thanks, but no thanks'.

Not only should I have made a positive decision, I should have made it very quickly, so that I could put a stop-loss on my worry. I should have said no the very moment I realised the job was wrong for me. I should have pulled away, irrespective of the (imagined) consequences. I realise now. I can see it all so clearly. The longer you leave it the harder it gets. And I should never have worried about what others thought of me. If you worry too much about what others think you'll probably never do anything. Also it is pretty naïve to think that people spend their entire lives making judgements about us, most people are too busy getting on with their own lives to even have the time to think about us. We are not mind-readers. We should not try to second-guess other people's thoughts. When we do we're usually wrong anyway. Especially during times of stress because paranoia is a noted side effect of tiredness and worry.

I should have used Dr Daniel G. Amen's 18-40-60 rule; at 18 we worry about what everyone is thinking about us, at 40 we don't care what everyone thinks of us and at 60 we realise no one has been thinking about us at all.

## The Sixty Per Cent Rule

Balance is very important in life, in fact it is imperative. Without balance we never feel quite right. Many people spend their lives aiming for a goal that'll make them happy when really they should be happy aiming for a goal. I spend my time being happy where I am whilst aiming for where I want to be. It is not the goal that makes you happy; it's getting there. Being happy is about being balanced. Working hard, yes, at times prolifically, but also rest hard and play hard too. Have a storming day at work but make sure that you spend time with those you love having fun and also give your body the rest it needs.

I wish I'd have known all this way back then. With hindsight as my greatest teacher I try to use only sixty per cent of my energy for achieving my life goal. Thirty per cent I use to play hard and have fun and the final ten per cent I leave in reserve for little emergencies that might happen along the way. If I do break this golden rule in an emergency and have to go over the edge of the U I make sure that I don't stay there too long. This way I never go into dangerous energy debt.

Work hard yes, of course, but always within the periphery of the sixty per cent. You'll be amazed at how much you can achieve if you use this sixty per cent well. Dipping into the other forty per cent is false economy; it might get you ahead of the game in the short-term but often to the detriment of all else, especially your health. I want to be successful in my life, I'm sure we all do, but I want to have a great time as well. If you think about it, enjoying your life is success; it just doesn't get any better than having a great time.

It's easy to start getting all one dimensional with regard to success. I don't measure my success by the amount of money in my bank. How successful am I as a son, as a husband or as a father? How successful am I as a friend or a neighbour? How well do I treat those around me who are of no profit?

If you just chase money then you'll probably get it but don't expect it to bring happiness if you are not happy already. Money is a transient and external security. Who you are and what you do for others is where true happiness lies, if money comes with it then it's a bonus. I like money, and God willing I will continue to make some but I will never allow it to become my God. I just refuse to let it define me.

One day I asked a lady of 80 what she had learned from her life thus far, what was important to her after a stay of eight decades. She said 'family and friends'. All the money and the possessions in the world don't mean much when you lose a husband of fifty years, a son of five years, a wife of ten years. Paul McCartney is one of the richest men on the planet, one of the very richest. And a very nice man too by all accounts. But do you think for a single second, for even one millisecond, he wouldn't swap every penny he owns for the life of his lovely wife Linda? He'd probably have given it over in a heartbeat.

We have to make a living, of course. Financial success? I heartily recommend it. But let's keep it all in perspective and have a great time on the way.

## Being Proactive

We were talking about the sixty per cent rule. As a youngster I over-trained and overworked myself – hard and very often – into illness and depression. And to be quite honest I didn't get that much further in life for all of it. It was like one step forward and one step back. That was because I didn't have a balanced outlook. I'd sprint and race, thinking that I was getting ahead only to realise that all I was getting was tired. And when I stopped to have a rest the whole lot caught up on me and I ended up back where I started. Now I work very hard, I get right ahead, then I have a rest before I get too tired, I play a little and have fun, then I start again. This way I get the maximum out of my body and at the same time I get the maximum out of life.

I discipline myself not to take on more than the sixty per cent; I avoid getting out of balance.

Be proactive and try to avoid problems before they occur. If you are living in an area where the neighbours are an irresolvable problem, move. Lose them. Lose them in a heartbeat! Lose the house, the street, lose the whole area if you have to and do it now before it affects who you are. It has already been medically proven that your influences affect your brain and subsequently your mood. Influences (good or bad) can change limbic activity in the brain. If your influences are negative it inflames the Limbic system leading to stress, anxiety and depression, if they are positive it cools the limbic system and gives you feelings of contentment and well being. If you were to have a SPECT scan of your brain you would be able to witness overactivity in the limbic part of the brain when influences are bad and the opposite when your influences are good. So change your influences if they are bad and don't let them mess with your limbic. Streets and houses are the semantics of life, being happy and content is real living, it's life; the rest is just environmental. Don't be tied to a house or a street, or an area. If you are happy you'll take joy with you wherever you go.

I lived in a bed-sit for about a year. It was the scummiest hole you ever set eyes on. My neighbours looked like serial killers. But I loved that place. I loved it because I shared it with Sharon, my wife (the one who puts my dinner on a plate instead of on my head). It was the roughest abode this side of a cardboard box, but it was filled with so much love that we were impervious to all else. It was a room full of love, which made it, to us, a world full of love. Eventually we moved to something bigger and then bigger again, but we never lost sight of the fact that when you have love you take it with you. If you are not happy where you are, make plans to live somewhere else, but at the same time remind yourself of who you are and what you've got. Enjoy the experience of where you are while you aim to get where you want to be. If you are not financially in a position to move right now, make plans to make it so. Our immediate environment can be one of our greatest influences, if it is a bad influence then change it. You're not running away, it's not cowardice or giving in, it's just being selective. Giving in, staying, is being cowardly because the ego says you should. If I was having problems with my neighbours and I felt the problem was beyond solving I'd move house and area in a hurry.

My friend had a constant problem with the family that lived next door to him. He hated the constant stress. Eventually it got so bad that it made him ill. I asked, 'why don't you move house, go to a nicer area?'

'I shouldn't have to do that,' he replied, 'I've got just as much right to live around here as they have. I'm not being chased away by them! It's wrong.'

I explained to him, it is not about what is right and wrong, it's about what is and what is not. We all know, and will all no doubt agree, that we have the right to live wherever we want but does that really make you want to live the rest of your life around a bunch of low lifes just because you have that right? I've got every right to go and live in the biggest scum hole in my city, and get attacked on a daily basis if I want to, but I choose not to because that is not how I want to live my life. Don't allow your pride or ego to get involved here, if you are not happy then either move, or make plans to do so, irrespective of what other people might think of you. Try to imagine that you didn't live where you are living right now, but were thinking of buying the property. Would you buy it and move in knowing what you know now?

My friend said 'I've lived here all of my life, I was brought up in this area, I don't want to move!'

As I said, home is wherever love resides, just because you move from one house to another does not mean that you are going to lose your happiness, that's something that you will take with you wherever you go. And if you really can't make the move then stop procrastinating and live with the problems you are facing. By not addressing a problem you automatically disqualify yourself from being able to complain about it. Be bold, make the decision and deal with it.

As far as the problem with the tax is concerned, open a tax account and put some money away each week to cover the next bill. This way you'll not be faced with the same problem perennially.

With work, try to keep ahead of yourself at all times. Don't allow your load to pile up. And be assertive, don't be a doormat for overbearing bosses who use you as a dustbin for extra work. Don't let them overload you with work that you cannot possibly cope with. If you are not an assertive person, learn to be by taking classes at the local college. Remember, if you don't do anything about it, you lose the right to complain. And please, don't blame others; they only do to us what we allow them to do. If you can't cope with the workload, or the attitude of the boss or the conditions, complain. If the supervisor doesn't listen, go to the boss, if he doesn't listen go above his head. Do what ever is necessary to make it so. How are they going to know you're not happy if you don't tell them? And if you are working for a company that does not listen, find yourself another company to work for that does. If it can't be changed (it always can) or you feel it can't, deal with it.

I am aware that the examples I have given are all relatively easy ones to solve. I'm aware that more problems than I have envisaged here might occur, but that's life (as Esther might say). There will always be problems to solve; the only place where we don't get any is down at the local cemetery, it's full of people with no more earthly problems at all. This leads me to believe that problems are good because they are a sign of life. One thing is for sure, there is always an answer even if it is not immediately forthcoming, but you won't find it if you don't look. Problems have a habit of getting bigger if you don't address them immediately. When you look the problems in the eye and set out to tackle them they'll fall apart like a cheap suit.

Whilst we live we will experience problems. We grow by meeting them maturely and bravely, then overcoming them.

Sometimes, if problems cannot be resolved, we may have to take more drastic measures.

My friend had a job that was just too demanding. He could cope but it left him with no energy for anything else in life. He was basically just working and sleeping and had little time or patience for his family. If he sat still for long enough he would either burst into tears or fall fast asleep – sometimes in the car on the motorway. He always associated crying with weakness, so every time he cried he got more stressed and every time he got more stressed he cried. He was on a downward spiral. He had a chat with his boss at work and tried to delegate some of his workload. His boss made all the right noises but things didn't change. He was left with no other option; he had to change jobs. This meant a large decrease in pay, which bothered him enough to delay his decision for a couple of months. That extra couple of months of worry took him over the edge of the U and into the red. He became very depressed and was on the verge of a nervous breakdown. It was only when, eventually, he made the decision and found another job that he gradually got back to black. Yes, the money was not so good but he was happy and light and that meant more to him than all the money in the world. He is now in a job he loves. It works for him and he also has the option of climbing the corporate ladder and making the same, and more, money as he was in his old, unhappy job.

We have two choices in this life, change what is wrong and make it right, or live with it and accept your lot. As a species we are creators, we have the ability to create, so if something is wrong in your life create a better world for you and those you love.

# Chapter Four
# We Always Hurt
# The Ones We Love

Why, as the song says, do we always seem to hurt the ones we love? The ones we love are the ones we shouldn't hurt at all. If we love them so much why do we take out our stress on them?

All of us at one time or another has probably been guilty of taking out our stress on those closest to us. We too have probably been the victims of similar displacement ourselves, when the ones that we love take out their stress on us.

My friend John displaced his stress on his lovely wife for many years. Deep down he knew he was in the wrong but rather than accept responsibility, he rationalised and projected the blame on to her. It was Jane's fault for being so irritating, for being late with his dinner, for driving too slow or for driving too fast, she was either too soft with the kids (in his opinion) or too hard. Jane was a lovely girl. She was very soft, which I think is a nice characteristic, but John took advantage of her nature and, subsequently, she took the abuse and the blame for many years. She never answered back and never stood up for herself. She became an easy target for his displacement. The reason she didn't argue back was because she didn't like confrontation, anything for a quiet life. But by not standing up to her bullying spouse she was telling him that what he was doing was OK, subsequently he did it all the more. She became submissive to avoid confrontation but her submissiveness drew confrontation her way. People, like dogs, are drawn and often attack when they sense fear. Jane became more and more anxious until she was on the verge of a breakdown. One morning, right out of the blue, she decided that she'd had enough and gave John the bad news. She told him at breakfast that she didn't love him any more and that, for her own sanity, she wanted a divorce. As you can imagine he was absolutely devastated. The unexpected news knocked him sideways. 'It was so sudden, and for no reason' he told me.

It wasn't sudden, and the reasons had been growing all their married life. He was the only one that couldn't see it. He had abused her so much it had killed what she felt for him. She simply stopped loving him. He did everything to rekindle the fire but it was well and truly out. She actually wanted to love him because she could see how much pain he was in, but she couldn't, it just wasn't there anymore.

It is easy here to place all the blame on John, he was the aggressor after all. But Jane also has a responsibility; she also, inadvertently, played her part. She allowed the abuse to happen because she felt uncomfortable with confrontation. And if she goes into other relationships with the same attitude, private or business, she'll probably get the same treatment. It'll stop when she refuses to take it anymore. Confrontation by its very nature is uncomfortable, but if you don't nip problems in the bud they have a habit of become fully-fledged fears.

I'm pleased to say that Jane learnt her lessons well and took them into a new relationship, she is now happily married to a very caring man. John never got over the breakup, he never learned his lessons. It wasn't his fault of course, he told me, it was Jane's.

Whether suppressed and held in, or expressed in a direct argument, negative displacement is bad news for any relationship. In the long-term it could kill it.

## Stress Can be a Gift

If negative displacement is so detrimental to relationships why do we still do it? Why do we continue to hurt those we love?

I don't think we mean to hurt them. There is no doubt that the abuse is wrong, but that doesn't mean it's deliberate. I think, nine times out of ten, it is inadvertent, that is, we don't know we're doing it. And if we do know we're doing it how can we stop it?

Negative stress release occurs because of the pressure cooker syndrome. It builds up inside to such an extent that eventually it has to blow its lid. It's a very physical thing; there is surplus energy and it has to go somewhere. Some people have learned to see this excess as a gift and drive it into their business. Many top CEOs of major companies are successful because they are more susceptible to stress, and rather than allow negative displacement to occur they use the energy and displace it positively into their work, that's why they are so prolific.

The reason the displaced abuse is perhaps unconscious is because we hide the real cause of our stress from a conscious mind that seems unable, or unwilling to deal directly with it. The hiding (or denial as it is officially known) is done via Freudian defence mechanisms. Rather than accept, and therefore deal with, the object of our stress (the core stressor – something we might be too scared to confront), we displace our tension on to some temporary object or person that our conscious mind can face. This might be our spouse, one of our children, a driver on the road, even an inanimate object like a door. We then rationalise our action to justify ourselves, by blaming the object we have attacked. This way (we feel) we don't have to deal with the core stressor.

At other times there might not be a genuine stressor, we might just be more susceptible to stress and collect it more readily than others. It is well known that some people are easy going, maybe even lethargic, and others are overactive, over-stressed and overdriven. I have problems myself sometimes with being overdriven. My sympathetic nervous system is very sensitive; subsequently I get rushes of adrenalin and other stress hormones very easily. This is good and bad. The negative by-product is that I get overexcited about things and end up loaded with adrenalin. The physical symptoms this can bring are anxiety, nervousness, (for some people and in extreme cases) panic attacks, negativity, fatalism, conflict avoidance, muscle tension and soreness, the shakes, fine motor problems, headaches, excessive motivation and in some cases Tourette's syndrome or tics.

The amount of energy this gives me is often overwhelming and if not checked and regularly released it clogs my system and makes life very uncomfortable. However I do have a handle on it and can usually keep it in check with regular relaxation, meditation or prayer to calm the brain and physical training to release excess energy. The positive side of all this is that the extra energy I get allows me to be very driven and prolific in whatever area I choose to work. I get lots of work done very quickly. If the energy is excessive and overwhelming I do exercises that allow me to calm the part of my brain (the basal ganglia system) that creates the excess. These exercises will be detailed in a later chapter. The beauty of all this is that, if you are under-motivated and depressive you can stimulate the basal ganglia system into action with specific techniques; if you are over motivated and always anxious you can calm it down with relaxation exercises and meditation. What I am trying to say here is that, just because you might have a predisposition one way or another does not mean that you are stuck that way for life. You can change the way your brain works by understanding how it works and make it better adapted for your world. For greater detail on this subject you need go no further than the amazing and groundbreaking book *Change Your Brain, Change Your Life* by Daniel G. Amen, MD.

Stressors, things that make us anxious or scared, cause stress. If these are not removed they can, and do, continue to cause us stress.

Julie's husband Jim, a successful journalist, took on a very stressful job as a war correspondent. Up until this point their relationship had been idyllic. Jim was gentle and considerate and Julie loved these qualities in a man.

Shortly after arriving home from his first trip to war-torn Bosnia their problems began. The old Jim had all but completely disappeared, only to be replaced by a very angry and explosively aggressive Jim who became expressively intolerant about almost everything. He would become angry with Julie over the slightest thing. She spilt a little red wine on the carpet one night by accident, and Jim called her 'stupid and incompetent'. He also became aggressive towards other road users whilst driving the car. Julie noticed his highly critical attitude towards some of their friends. And if she dared to defend them she was (he claimed) on their side, and Jim would become sulky, often for days on end.

When Julie approached him about his mood swings he denied that anything was wrong and told her that she should look closer to home if she wanted to find the problems with their relationship. He projected all the blame on to her, saying it was she who had changed. He was even worse when under the influence of alcohol.

When Julie and I last spoke, she was at her wits' end and on the verge of leaving him. She was frightened he might become violent; his outbursts were becoming more frequent and more aggressive.

I'd like to tell you that they survived his displacement but I can't. Last I heard things had got worse. She'd suggested to Jim that he see a doctor and that his problem might be stress related but he wouldn't have it. He not only refused to take responsibility; he wouldn't even talk about it.

## Reaction Formation

Another friend Dick (now a very highly graded martial arts instructor), dealt with his denial using Reaction Formation. Dick had a strong fear of entering karate tournaments. He couldn't consciously admit his fear because he felt he'd lose respect if people thought he was scared. Rather than admit his fear when the subject of competition arose, he vehemently attacked it instead. He told his fellow martial artists that he was against sport karate, that it was bad for the martial aspect of his art, that's why he wouldn't enter a competition. He convinced his friends, and for a while he even convinced himself. To hide his fear of competition (from himself as much as from others) he attacked competition.

## Layering of Stress

For those of us living stressful lives there tends to be a layering of stress that occurs over a day, a week, a month sometimes even over a whole lifetime. In these cases it's only a matter of time before a natural overflow occurs. When the dam is ready to burst it doesn't take much to trigger it, and when it does burst it destroys everything in its path.

The body needs a release for stress. This much we have established. But our conscious sentry (the superego), a mental guard that keeps us aware of social rights and wrongs, keeps this displacement under lock and key until a safe opportunity arises. If a safe release is not forthcoming, or if a person has little self-control, this release will occur whether socially acceptable or not.

This amounts to negative displacement and generally seems to occur when the conscious sentry is switched off, weakened, distracted or, in the case of people with little or no social conscience, at any time.

To those with a social conscience it can be when we relax into the safety of our own homes, when distracted in the car or under the weakening influence of alcohol or drugs (when we drink or take drugs we tend to give the internal parent – or common sense – a night off).

We displace our stress in the home because this is where we relax; our social guard is down. In public people often wear a nice mask because society demands a certain protocol if the right impression is to be made. In the home however the mask comes off (a degree of familiarity has usually occurred in many relationships) and no such pretence has to be observed.

Everyone at the pub thought Steve was a lovely man, a real laugh. He had a reputation of a man who would do anything for anyone. At home it was a different story. At home, where his social mask was placed in a cupboard with his coat and hat Steve was an absolute grouch. He wouldn't lift a finger to help his wife or children. And if he did he moaned and complained all the way through the task. His kids were actually frightened of him and his wife was constantly on a knife's edge because of his irritability and explosive temper.

Understanding negative displacement is the first step to stopping it from happening, but it will take discipline and self-control to put the information to work.

## Telltale Signs of Imminent Displacement

There are usually telltale signs when displacement is imminent. If you can spot these pre-cursors you can stop the negative displacement before it starts. Watch out for the signs. I normally become fidgety or irritable over little or nothing, I find myself looking for arguments or being snappy with people. When I look at my wife and feel angry just because she's there, that's normally a bad sign. Or when my appetite is suppressed or increased or I can't sleep properly at night, or perhaps I am sleeping too much, these are signs of stress build up. Also, when I find myself being critical about others, or shouting at inanimate objects it is a bad sign. If I start feeling as though other people don't like me, or imagine that they are speaking about me behind my back, general paranoia, again I know that the dam is about to burst and I do something about it. These are just some of the general signs that I notice in my own pre-displacement. Spotting the signs enables you to do something about it.

My first action when stressed is to find a way to get the stress out of me before it explodes and upsets people. A Safe Surrogate Release (more details in a later chapter) that will work the stress out of my system physically. If this is not available, or immediately appropriate for whatever reason, I'll click into self-control and hold back any temper or irritability that I might feel.

If I am at work, and I feel irritable and want to vent my anger on someone (or something) I control myself and do the exact opposite. I spot the early warning signs and consciously control my emotions until a safe release is available. The very act of noticing your own stress signs allows you to slow everything down and take control, even to the point of being more patient and considerate than usual. When I feel like shouting at the whole world I consciously do the opposite. I take more time with the people around me, I even make a point of telling them they are doing a great job, and if they mess something up I'll say something like 'Don't worry, it won't change the course of our lives.'

I remember one such occasion, standing in a rather long supermarket queue one busy Friday afternoon. I was doing a bit of shopping after a stressful day. The girl at the checkout was taking (or at least is seemed so in my agitated state) an eternity with everyone's shopping. I felt in my paranoiac state that she was doing it on purpose. I remember thinking 'blimey, if she slows down any more she'll stop. Why is she so slow?' I could feel my anger building and I began fidgeting and looking impatiently at my watch. I was sighing impatiently, rolling my eyes and tutting. I did everything bar shout out loud 'hurry up!'

The checkout girl was getting visibly frustrated at the impatience of myself and the rest of the queue. She was looking very stressed and unhappy. In an instant I caught myself in the very beginnings of displacement. I spotted the signs; they were almost chalked across my angry brow. I countered all the little negative thoughts that were racing, unchallenged, through my mind, with positive thoughts. I swatted them like flies. I reminded myself that this was not about the checkout girl, it was about my stressful day. I was about to displace myself (for want of a better expression) on an innocent girl, trying to do an honest day's work. I took a deep breath in through my nose (diaphragmatic breathing; this triggers the parasympathetic nervous system and calms you down) and consciously calmed myself. For an instant I slowed down my whole world. I told myself 'there's no real hurry'. Life would still be there when I got home, whether I was running late or not. And even if I were in a hurry, my impatience wouldn't make the checkout girl go any faster, quite the opposite in fact. My stress, displaced on to her, would make her stressed and all the fine motor actions needed to work the checkout keyboard would be made redundant. She'd probably slow to a halt, and then I might not get through the queue before my next birthday. I stopped thinking about how long this lovely young lady was taking with the shopping in front of me and began appreciating the things around me. I started 'people watching'; observing mannerisms and quirks and smiling if people caught my eye. Then I laughed (to myself). The irony was funny. I had caught myself out, and as a result was able to exercise a little self-control over a part of me that usually worked all by itself. When I got to the front of the queue I looked at the checkout girl. She was still very stressed. For a second I visualised myself in her place and appreciated what a good job she was doing under such pressure. I said to her, 'you know what, I really admire the way you're dealing with all this stress, you're very professional. I just wanted to say that I appreciate you'.

You should have seen the smile on her face. As I walked away I heard her passing some polite conversation to the next customer.

### Let Them In On It

Another great trick, one I find works for me (especially at home), is to tell people when you feel a displacement coming on. When you feel like snapping someone's head off let them in on it. It's amazing how the feelings of anger and displacement dissipate when you do this. When I feel tense I just say to my wife, 'I'm sorry if I'm a little tense I feel really stressed, I feel like I'm going to explode. It's not you, it's me, I've had a real stressful day'. Then I give her a big hug and a kiss.

Once I've done this I always feel better. The stress just melts away. Not only do I feel good for sharing my woes but also the very fact that I have admitted fault brings the whole thing to a conscious level. It stops defensive projection (pushing the blame on to others). How can I blame others when I have just admitted fault? I can hardly project or displace my stress on to my wife unconsciously once I have admitted consciously that it's not her fault.

## Put a Stop-loss on the Hurt

Letting others in on my stress is a proactive technique I use for stopping negative displacement. But what if you've already displaced or projected? What do you do once the damage has already been done?

What I do is stop it as soon as possible, this limits damage. This is as much for me as it is for the displacee. I will grip the feelings of anger or irritability and hold them back and, again, apologise to the person I have upset or got angry with, whoever that might be, and admit fault. I will also tell them why I feel so irritable and angry. People appreciate honesty, I am never too proud to be honest or to say sorry.

I believe it was Lynn Johnston who said 'an apology is the superglue of life. It can repair just about anything'.

But do it soonest, the longer an apology goes unsaid the more damage is incurred.

If the situation has already occurred and the damage done it is never too late to break out the flowers and chocolates and, again, admit fault – unreservedly. And don't forget apologies, it is not enough to just feel sorry, you have to say it. It'll mend many a bruised heart. I've apologised to people I upset five years ago. I've bumped into them in the street, or at training, and said 'do you remember five years ago when I upset you, well I realise now I was completely out of order and I just wanted to say I'm sorry.'

Don't expect forgiveness, if they don't want to forgive (some people are not capable) then accept it, it's their prerogative, although if they do forgive you that's a bonus. If you do apologise make it sincere and unreserved or not at all. One of my friends apologised to his wife saying very bluntly, 'I'm sorry if I upset you, I had a stressful day, and you just wind me up.' That's a half-apology, in fact it's more blame than it is apology. On another occasion he said to her, 'I'm sorry if I upset you and I want to make up but if you want to keep up this silly silent treatment then fine, I'm not going to beg you.'

That's not an apology either, it's a threat. Either apologise completely, or don't bother at all. You can no sooner half-apologise than you can half-dig a hole in the ground.

Another chap whose displacement was always physically violent, said to me, 'I'm in therapy. I know I've got a bad temper Geoff but some girls ask for it don't they, they just wind you up, they need a slap!'

Great therapy! Make it sincere or not at all.

## Road Rage

Another area of displacement (and I know we did a bit of this earlier) is in the car when the sentry is distracted, or tunnelled. The sentry is often so occupied with driving the car and not having a crash (almost in a mild state of hypnosis when the unconscious mind is easily accessible) that it leaves an opening for negative displacement. If you have a lot of stress in your life, and no physical release, it's only a matter of time until the pressure blows the lid off your self-control. This doesn't explain why some people resort to road rage whilst others do not. The people prone to road rage are most likely those with overactivity in the cingulate system in the brain (people who are biologically easily stressed – it's how they're made as my mum might say). This can make some people more anxious than others, and therefore more inclined to lose their tempers in the car. These types struggle to release negative thought from their minds, they get stuck on certain emotions that will loop around and around their brains. They often worry to the point of causing emotional and physical harm to themselves or others. In road rage this type gets locked into the negative thoughts associated with someone cutting them up on the road or cutting in front of them in traffic. Subsequently they may be less able to control their frustration, often to the point of driving dangerously to get back in front of the car that cut them off or chasing the car for miles off their route. Or even – as in the case of a successful business executive with cingulate problems – getting out of his vehicle and hitting the doors of the other vehicle with a baseball bat that he carried in the car for just such occasions.

## The Pressure Cooker Effect

Some time ago I myself was the victim of road rage. I was driving my car home from a visit to the bank when the duel carriageway filtered into one lane. I was in the outside lane trying to filter into the inside lane. As soon as I got into the inside lane the driver in the van behind me, obviously unhappy because I had got one space ahead of him in the traffic, started to beep, shook his fist and screamed at me out of the window. I understood what was occurring so I took no notice. He then spent the next ten minutes trying to get back in front of me, driving very dangerously to do so. Eventually he shot right in front of me, shook his fist angrily out of the window and then raced off never to be seen again. I could have made this problem worse by getting angry right back, but instead I just smiled at him and went on my merry way, no worse for the experience. My understanding of why this man acted the way he did enabled me to be patient with him and not take it personally.

As we said earlier, these types are more sensitive to stress because their brain activity makes them more prone to stressors than a person with normal brain activity. So they collect more stress hormones throughout the day than the average person. This is one of the reasons why, when I see someone ranting at me from their car I don't think 'idiot!' and give him aggro back, I think 'cingulate system!' and congratulate myself on having noticed. The real danger of course is if the two drivers involved in a traffic incident (or any incident for that matter) are both cingulate sensitive. That's when the sparks really start to fly and, in many cases, it manifests into actual physical violence, sometimes even murder.

This doesn't mean that if you are cingulate sensitive you can't do anything about it. You are not at the mercy of your hormones. With specific exercises in breathing, positive thinking, self-control and internal dialogue (in some cases specific medication) you can control it and make it work for you. As I said, many top CEOs are basal ganglia or cingulate Sensitive, but they control and harness their energy and make it work for them very successfully.

On the flip side of the coin many potential CEOs fail to control the force and end up either becoming overwhelmed by the stress and pull away, mistaking the feelings for fear, or they displace their stress negatively and end up unhappy, often violent and sometimes in jail. I'd bet my pants that many of the violent people in our jails today are oversensitive in the cingulate system or basal ganglia.

We'll look at the control exercises later in the book.

People commit the most heinous crimes of violence over seemingly unimportant incidents. One driver was so angry and aroused after a week of 'tremendous stress' at work, he hit a pedestrian over the head with a hammer. And all because the old fellow didn't thank the driver for stopping and allowing him across the road. When he hammered his hapless victim into a bloody unconsciousness he was heard to say, 'that'll teach you not to say thank you, you ungrateful bastard!'

In another incident a motorcycle courier was so incensed when a female motorcyclist nipped past him in traffic, he dragged her off her bike by the neck, ripped her helmet off and then proceeded to punch her in the face. In court he told the judge he'd been highly stressed and blew his top when the lady cut in front of him. I could illustrate the point all day long, but I think you get it.

In the car the conscious sentry is distracted. It is even possible that we see our own car as an extension of the home and unconsciously switch off our social sentry. Also, our consciousness is focused so intently on one point, driving the car, we are almost in a meditative or hypnotic state. Have you ever got into the car and then suddenly found yourself three miles down the road with no memory of consciously getting there? This is a mild hypnotic state. The usual self-control we exercise in daily life is lowered and build-ups of stress find their way out. Sometimes this can result in beeped horns, shaken fists or verbal abuse. This in itself may not be drastic; it's when other drivers react badly to our outbursts (or us to theirs) that fists start to fly. Then you do have cause for concern.

When you feel the wild rush of road rage taking over – stop! Remember that it isn't him you're angry with; he's simply a displacement figure for the stress backlog. Similarly, he's probably not really angry with you either. It's not about either of you, it is about stress displacement. Similarly, when you get home from work and find yourself ranting and raving at the wife or the kids (or shouting at the telly) – stop! Remind yourself that it is not them, it's your boss, your heavy work schedule, deadlines that you can't meet, the puncture in your car, the rush-hour traffic – eureka! It's the stress.

The list goes on, but the point remains: when the guard is down, negative displacement will out. So beware.

## Alcohol and Drugs

Another dangerous time is when under the influence of alcohol or drugs. Ironically many people use alcohol as a stress suppressant. It often has the completely opposite effect. I can honestly say that the majority of fights I got into as a doorman were mostly caused by displacement, me being the manifestation of somebody else's woes, or, at times, them being the manifestation of mine. When alcohol comes in through the door, self-control goes out through the window. Some stimulants will make you feel better for a short while but it effectively puts the sentry to sleep and leaves you wide open for massive displacement. Also, withdrawal from alcohol causes anxiety and places a person already with anxiety at more risk from alcohol addiction.

As a doorman I could understand displacement and, to a degree, take it into account when someone tried to take it out on me. But the fact that it might not be personal, and I didn't take it personally, didn't always make the individual any less dangerous. His displacement was usually taking place unconsciously, and to him you are the problem not the outlet. And often no amount of communication will convince him otherwise. He doesn't know anything about displacement; he blames you, so you become the object of his aggression.

Little Johnny might be a nice chap normally, despite the fact that he is your archetypal 'stressed man.' He goes to the shops for the old lady next-door, and is always very polite; it's only when he drinks he gets a bit naughty. Is that going to stop him from pushing a broken beer glass in my face when sees me as a manifestation of all his woes? Probably not. I think at the moment I ask him to leave the nightclub for playing up, little Johnny is going to be the most dangerous person in my world. He might kill me, even if unintentionally.

So, even though I may understand displacement, and this knowledge will help me, it isn't going to count for much once Johnny has decided to take me out. This is the same if you are facing an irate shopper or driver. If communication is failing, make a hasty exit, call the police (or if you have the skill and no option to escape or call the police, prepare to defend yourself) because your life may be at risk.

My friend Tim, a fellow doorman, was so stressed over his marital problems he decided to have a drink to drown his sorrows. He had a couple and felt like a new man, but then the new man wanted a drink. And so it went on into the night until Tim (and all the new men) was very tipsy. He'd drunk the town dry as they say. Towards the end of the evening an argument ensued between Tim and a stroppy customer. It was just a standard dispute really, nothing out of the ordinary, but Tim took it personally and became incensed. He smashed his antagonist over the head with a baseball bat – four times. The customer became the manifestation of Tim's marital problems and a bloodied, battered mess.

Of course, as stated earlier, this is not the answer; it creates more stress than it releases. Life is a reciprocal experience, we are constantly getting what we have given. In this case it gave Tim many years of intense stress (and four years later a terrible beating when he bumped into the same man and four of his friends in a local bar). It turned out that the customer he hit with the bat was very well connected with some nasty people. He came back to the pub later that night (head stitched up like a football) with 40 of his very best friends (all with bats of their own) and smashed the place to matchsticks. Tim escaped, but only just. He had to leave his job on the door, and was still receiving death threats two years later. This was the beginning of the end for Tim; the pressure and constant stress emptied him. He has never regained his confidence. A few other heavy stressors over the next couple of years proved to be his *coup de grâce*. He tried to commit suicide twice, though thankfully he failed.

Once you understand the mechanics of displacement you possess the power to make positive changes, clean up any mess you may have made with sincere apologies and explanations, and then strive not to make the same mistakes again. You get to stop hurting the ones you love, which means you also get to stop hurting yourself.

# Chapter Five
# What Causes Stress?

The causes of stress are manifold and vary from individual to individual. One person might feel comfortable with something that another is very stressed or even fearful about. The causes of stress depend almost entirely upon individual perception and, to say the least, are very subjective. Stress cannot be adequately defined within a text, though a general outline of the majority of life stressors might prove useful.

We spoke briefly earlier about how people with overactive areas of the brain (cingulate system and basal ganglia) are genetically prone to higher stress levels, and how this has both good and bad points. People with heightened basal ganglia or cingulate system tend to work excessive hours and often achieve great things with their lives. The same people though, are notoriously bad at sitting and relaxing. Weekends tend to be difficult times for these types. They often complain of feeling restless, anxious and out of sorts. They find relaxation very uncomfortable and often end up not resting at all, even working through the weekend. This might make them more productive but it doesn't allow them quality time with their family. This can often end in arguments and even divorce. Also, they allow no recuperation time for the body and mind which, in the long-term, is very unhealthy. This is because the excess energy that drives them through tremendous workloads tends to collect during rest periods. The best way to take the top off this, to make it more manageable, is to take up a sport or a physical hobby. This gives the excess energy a surrogate battle until you get back to work. If you involve your family in these activities then you are also taking care of home life at the same time. Remember, all these stress hormones rushing around your body amount to little more than energy that you can use as a fuel for anything you like. It doesn't care what you use it for as long as you use it. Even if someone really upsets you, to the point of making you very angry. If you strip the emotions from the anger, what are you left with? Fuel. I know many people who have succeeded in life purely because someone told them they wouldn't. They were so incensed and angry at these people that they went out to prove them wrong, and every time they get tired and lack energy they simply think about what this person said and Bang! They're totally refuelled again.

## Why Criticism and Insult Can be a Gift

In my early days of writing I had many critics who were aggressively against me. Their criticism initially angered me until I realised that every insult they threw created an energy within me that could be refined and used as a source of fuel to drive me towards my goals. As long as I didn't allow the insults to become personal and overwhelm me. What they were sending in effect was a gift, not very nicely packaged I have to say, but once the offending wrappers were stripped away it was a gift nonetheless. I was left with a lovely bundle of energy that I could (and frequently did) use in my quest for success. So to all of those people that made it their job to criticise me (you know who you are) I say thank you – and keep it coming. It's as good as money in the bank. As far as I'm concerned energy is currency, it's what allows me to make my living so it is almost as though these people were sending me cash in the post (the fools). Try to remember this when others get you angry or stressed; it's not personal, it's a gift, recognise it and use it. You will forget though, I do from time to time. Just keep reminding yourself and you will never lack the fuel to get where you want to go. And also remind yourself that if you don't take this gift and make the mistake of reacting with aggression you are not only missing out on a gift, you are also sending your critics money in the post because you are giving them your energy (now you don't want to be doing that). Once you are in receipt of the energy you must do something with it, use it with a very strong work ethic and drive it into your business or life. Don't become bitter about the criticism; don't wish to be successful just to hurt others. Forgive them and make a gift of the energy they send you otherwise you carry them around like a heavy sack on your back. For more on handling criticism please refer to *The Elephant and the Twig*, which has a good chapter on this subject.

Suffice to say that, within reason, almost anything can be a stressor if it is deemed as stressful to the person involved. Some might feel very comfortable facing extreme violence every night of the week working as a nightclub doorman, and yet having a mortgage, or making a commitment to a partner might frighten them so much that they can't cope. I have a close friend, a former soldier, who has seen active service in the forces, and coped very well in life-threatening situations. Yet news of his girlfriend's unexpected pregnancy left him feeling extremely apprehensive. He was genuinely frightened; in fact he struggled to deal with it.

Another friend, Pete, was a proper blood-and-snot street fighter, he would have it with anyone and seemed fearless as far as violent encounters were concerned. And yet the thought of holding a mortgage frightened him so much that it ended his marriage. Ironically the stress hormones released in both scenarios are identical, it is only knowledge – or lack of – that deems one *controllable* stress ('I am a fighter, skilled in combat and I know how to deal with a physical confrontation') and the other *uncontrollable* stress ('I know nothing about holding a mortgage and the thought of it, the long-term commitment, frightens the pants off me'). So it is lack of information, an exaggeration of the information you do hold, or even the fact that the information you have been given is false, that creates fear. Paradoxically, when you do have all the information the fear often dissipates because fear is a shadow, and information is light. When you shine a light on a shadow it disappears. If you do have all the information, it is correct and not exaggerated and it still frightens the pants off you, then confronting that particular stressor becomes a calculated risk that you may or may not wish to take.

A skydiver, for instance, knows the dangers he faces when he jumps out of a plane. He makes it his job to get as much information about skydiving as he can, so as to lower the danger but, all said and done, there is still a calculated risk that he chooses to take. The rewards (in his eyes) outweigh the risks. If he felt that the risks outweighed the rewards then he probably wouldn't be jumping out of aeroplanes with nothing more for safety than a large umbrella. So the risk/reward relationship is completely subjective, but the more information you have, the easier it is to see clearly what the risks are – if indeed there are any at all. Often information completely dispels fear – and therefore helps you come to a decision.

There are as many stressors as there are people and each is as different as the person perceiving it. We all look through different eyes, and see life threats, or perceived life threats, in a totally different and unique way. So when we talk about the causes of stress we must be patently aware of individuality.

Most people's perception of stress is of an event or experience whose demands exceed their coping capacity - even taking into account the whole range of individual perceptions to the same event. Many people may find divorce a stressful life event for instance, but all for different reasons. Having said that, anything that stops us from actually achieving our goals is a possible source of stress, even a traffic jam that stops us reaching a destination (which in this case is the goal) can cause tremendous stress.

Frustration, again a form of stress, is generally defined as being some kind of negative emotional state that occurs when we are prevented from reaching a goal. But what causes frustration? Frustration usually results when the brain cannot distinguish between a real source of physical threat and an imagined threat, so it prepares for both as though they were real. It does this by releasing stress hormones to arouse the body for a physical action.

It would be true to say that it is often our own inadequacies which prevent us from achieving our goals and ambitions. For example, we might dream of being a professional football player even though we perhaps haven't developed the talents to back up that dream and make it a reality. Or perhaps we would like to be a nurse but can't stand the sight of blood. There are also external, environmental factors over which we have little or no control that can also be the source of our stress if we allow them to. Things like the telephone being out of order when we need to make an urgent call, or the train being late when we are on the way to work or an important meeting. These are things that are outside the circle of our immediate influence, they cannot be changed, and yet we still allow them to become a great source of anxiety and frustration. We expend untold amounts of energy procrastinating (even if it is only internally) about things that are beyond our control. Again this would be like sitting at traffic lights in the car, pushing the accelerator to floor without engaging the clutch. Lots of noise, lots of wasted petrol but still no further forward.

So conflict is the main source of our stress, even if it's just being stuck in traffic.

## Conflict

Stress may also develop when a person experiences two – or possibly more – competing or contradictory motives or goals.

This can be 'approach-approach' conflict, where we are forced to choose between two equally attractive alternatives. This often happens in cases of infidelity when a person is forced to choose between two lovers, both of whom are equally attractive in different ways. Anxiety in this case stems from the inability to choose which partner is most favourable. Often the indecision is so long lasting the person loses both options.

This happened with a friend of mine who had a beautiful and adoring wife and an equally beautiful mistress. He kept his wife in the dark about his affair for many years. At the same time he kept his mistress on the hook by promising that he would leave his wife – soon. Both women were so appealing to him and he couldn't make the decision to be with one over the other. Basically he wanted to have his cake and eat it. Eventually his mistress got fed up of waiting and made the decision for him, she went off with someone else. Coincidentally, at the very same time, his wife found out about the affair and left him also. The dog that chases two rabbits usually catches neither. On a lesser scale the conflict may be between two different college courses, both of which look equally inviting, making it very difficult to choose one over the other. It is in this period of indecision that conflict blooms and energy levels dissipate.

Next we have the 'avoidance-avoidance' conflict, which involves having to choose between two equally *unattractive* options, the best of a bad lot as they say. It is often a case of having to choose between the Devil and the deep blue sea. Things like choosing between living with a particularly uncomfortable health problem and having an operation to get it sorted out. Or choosing between a safe, but unsatisfying, job and a more exciting though perhaps precarious alternative. Both choices are equally bad, but until a choice is made the source of conflict remains.

Many people spend their entire lives in this state of conflict and indecision, never happy with their lot, but never quite bold or brave enough to face the elements and change.

Thirdly we have the 'approach-avoidance' conflict, which involves a person or situation having both desirable and undesirable qualities. For instance, wanting to study for a master's degree at university but at the same time wanting or needing to work and earn some cash for the finer things.

Like my friend Tim. He desperately wanted to train as a full-time judo player and fight on the national squad. But this would have meant giving up his full-time job, and subsequently losing money. This was a constant source of frustration to Tim because he wanted to be a full-time trainer, but not enough to lose money from work to get it. He said to me, 'a judo black belt won't pay my bills!'

## Make a Decision

If you sit and think about it I am sure that you could come up with a lot more examples of conflict resulting in stress. The important point is that stress comes from conflict that is born from indecision. The longer you take to make the decision, the worse the stress becomes. Eventually, if you leave it long enough, it also becomes self-perpetuating because stress begets stress. The worry and heavy contemplation experienced when trying (or failing) to make a decision over a long period empties the mental and physical fuel tanks; this then becomes a stressor in itself.

This survey taken in 1967 (Holmes and Rache) shows a scale of events most stressful to most people. Even events we most look forward to, holidays, moving house, marriage, can still be very stressful.

1) Death of a spouse
2) Divorce
3) Marital separation
4) Jail term
5) Death of a close family member
6) Personal injury or illness
7) Marriage
8) Fired at work
9) Marital reconciliation
10) Retirement
11) Change in health of family member
12) Pregnancy
13) Sex problems
14) Gain a new family member
15) Business readjustment
16) Change in financial state
17) Death of a close friend
18) Change to a different line of work

19) Change in number of arguments with spouse

20) Mortgage over £10,000 (1967)

21) Foreclosure of a mortgage or loan

22) Change in responsibilities at work

23) Son or daughter leaving home

24) Trouble with the in-laws

25) Outstanding personal achievement

26) Partner begins or stops work

27) Begin or end school

28) Change in living conditions

29) Revision of personal habits

30) Trouble with boss

31) Changes at work

32) Change of residence

33) Change of schools

34) Change in recreation

35) Change in church activities

36) Change in social activities

37) Mortgage or loan less than £10,000

38) Change in sleeping habits

39) Change in number of family get-togethers

40) Change in eating habits

41) Holiday

42) Christmas

43) Minor violations of the law

This chart is very useful in that it allows us to recognise and identify common stressors. It doesn't cover every point of stress, only the major life stresses. But then, as I said earlier, how can it? Everything has the potential to be, or become, a stressor. To someone that is already highly stressed, a dripping tap can be enough to make him explode in anger. And the tendency is for stressed people to attract more stress, or certainly see non-stress items – things that would not usually bother them – as suddenly stressful. Many everyday occurrences, like gaining weight, misplacing or losing items, the rising price of merchandise, even a fictional character on the TV (I know loads of people who shout and get angry at images on the TV screen) are all stressors in their own right. Though singularly many of them are not overbearing, collectively they can be devastating.

## Comfort Zone

The majority of stressors share a common point; they all affect the individual's comfort zone. Anything that affects the comfort zone is a potential stressor, because it generally means change and growth or adjustment, which causes conflict, which in turn creates stress. The quicker we can accept these changes and move on, the less time we will spend in a stressed condition. If you can change your perception and see change as a challenge rather than a threat, life becomes an exciting ride not a runaway train.

By all means add your own stressors to the stress list if they are not there already. If it causes you grief it belongs on the list. Often we like to look at lists written in books so that we can put a name to our problems; putting a name to something does tend to give us a certain amount of power over it. I know when I was in a highly stressed condition I found great solace in naming my aches and pains. Seeing them on a stress list showed me I was not on my own, desperately ill, going mad, or all three. Paradoxically, if my symptoms were not on the list it often had the opposite effect. I felt alone, like no one else in the world felt as bad as I did or that my aches might be the first sign of something terminal (no, not an airport lounge). I realise now of course we're all very individual and we all experience stress in different ways. So don't worry if you are not up there on my list, believe me, you will be on someone's list.

# Chapter Six
# Who is Prone to Stress?

We are all prone to stress in varying degrees. By the very nature of our species, we are all likely to suffer the negative effects of adrenalin at one time or another. It is actually a built-in unconscious survival mechanism that has been a part of our make-up since man first roamed the earth with animal-hide pants and an ugly club. Of course the degree to which we experience stress, and what we perceive as being stressful, varies very much from individual to individual.

One probability for this is that behaviour and perceptions are learned responses from childhood. Another is that genetically some are more prone to stress than others, or it might be completely consistent with our environment. When I worked as a nightclub doorman my life was one of constant stress, but when I changed the environment, by changing my job, my stress levels fell to almost zero. From my experience stress comes from all of the above, our genetics, our upbringing and our environment.

There have been many studies on stress and the human response, and also on the types of people who experience extreme stress. The studies established that the main categories of people in society, as pertaining to stress, are either Type 'A' personality (highly driven, ambitious, stressed people) or Type 'B' personality (easy going, not easily stressed people).

It is thought that probably 80 per cent of the population is mild to moderate Type 'A' personality (moderately stressed), and ten per cent of the population is extreme Type 'A' personality (extremely stressed). The remaining ten per cent are probably Type 'B' personality (not very stressed).

Even though the 'B's are not highly stressed people it does not necessarily follow that they are not ambitious, many of them are, and highly successful too. But the way they achieve their success would be quite different from their Type 'A' counterparts.

Type 'A' personalities are highly competitive and ambitious people who are desperate to achieve ever-increasing and ever-demanding goals. When they reach one pinnacle they are never satisfied and quickly aim for another, more difficult goal, usually at the expense of everything and anything else in their lives – even their families. This is where they would differ from ambitious Type 'B's who would similarly aim for ever increasing goals – that is how success is made – but they would enjoy their life en route and balance their ambition with the needs of their family and the needs of their bodies. To rationalise this behaviour many 'A's say they are 'doing it for the family' and not for themselves. However rationalised it still tends to be at the expense of quality time with the family.

'A's appear impatient and hurried and are always conscious of time as though it is slipping through their fingers at every delay. Even a moment that is not tangibly productive is a minute (in their eyes) wasted. This can be false economy, their Type 'B' counterparts are often more successful and happier because of their delegating skills and the fact that they rest and play as hard as they work.

'A's feel more is better and to succeed in life we have to suffer. 'B's on the other hand believe that sometimes less is better and that it is quality that counts more than quantity. If there is no rest and no play the quality of every working day diminishes and a trap door to the downward spiral opens. 'A's are out of balance, 'B's are very balanced, in fact their whole life is about balance.

## Less is Sometimes Better

As a young martial artist I had the notion (and it took me a long time to get this out of my head) that I had to kill myself in training to get any results. And I reached quite a decent level with this method, though not the heights I aspired to and not without many injuries and setbacks. I literally did the physical bit to death and lost much time due to the injuries and illness incurred en route. I eventually reached an impasse in my training where injury and illness stopped me dead in my tracks. I just couldn't seem to improve beyond the standard I had reached, no matter how many hours I trained. It was then that I stumbled on the truth: I was all quantity and little quality. If I wanted to reach my Everest I realised that I had to make quality my goal. This meant changing who I trained with, where I trained, what I ate, my influences: everything. I started training fewer hours, but made the new regime one of meticulous quality. It was also imperative that I had time away from training; rest and play became just as important, because most bodily repairs (often a grossly over-looked factor) take place during rest and play.

In my business life I started to trust others and delegated wherever and whenever possible. This left me with more energy to achieve excellent results in the things I did undertake. I started working fewer hours, but being more productive whilst I did work. I disciplined myself to stop when I said I would and not work deep into the night in the belief that I might get more done. My martial arts and my writing went to a standard I'd never achieved before and my business boomed.

I didn't feel like I was doing as much as I should (because of my old paradigm) but, looking at the results, I had actually achieved more than ever before. In the four months between January and April of that year I completed seven new books, as well as dozens of magazine articles. Because my hours were shorter I spent many a happy afternoon having tea and a cake in the town with my wife, something I looked forward to immensely.

Type 'A's unfortunately do not see it this way, they are constantly looking to control their environment and are preoccupied with (self-imposed) deadlines and are very intolerant of any kind of delay. They are often hostile and driven, but generally this is internal rather than external. They are usually unable or unwilling to express their emotions, feelings or anger outwardly or directly. Their verbal battles and screaming and shouting are more likely to take place in their own minds. If their feelings are expressed externally it is most likely to manifest itself on the squash court or in the swimming baths. Even leisure for the Type 'A's becomes a game of survival where they go all out to win.

Anthony is a type 'A' personality. When he took up golf for a bit of light, therapeutic exercise, he allowed his game to become competitive rather than leisurely. Before long he was smashing a golf club over his knee when he made a bad shot.

Type 'A's tend to set unrealistic goals and targets for themselves, subsequently triggering the race with time and the failure to cram fat workloads into slim (self-imposed) timeframes. Thus failure to complete tasks, and subsequent feelings of failure for not having done so, are inevitable. These create self-doubt and self-loathing (ego) and, of course, stress perpetuation. Harder work regimes are then set to make up for lost time.

So generally Type 'A's take on more that they can realistically cope with which has them constantly chasing time. Their whole lives are lived in a blur, with no time to stop and smell the roses. They will invariably use any and every defence mechanism to justify their actions and very rarely realise the quandary they are in. Because of the self-imposed, unrealistic workloads and deadlines, and the fact that they tend to take on too much at any one time, Type 'A's never seem to complete a task fully before moving on to the next. This generates stress and their subsequent irritation and anger often surfaces (eventually if not immediately) over the most trivial matters. They also tend to blow these matters completely out of proportion. Because they do not consciously recognise their Type 'A' status they rarely apologise for their outbursts, preferring instead to project the blame on to others. Which of course leaves a trail of resentment and bad energy in their wake.

Attention to detail, numbers, quantities and general accuracy tend also to become obsessions, making it difficult for them to delegate because they believe that no one can do the job quite as well as them. If they do delegate work they do not do it well, constantly checking and fault finding in the work of their employees.

The conversation of the Type 'A' tends to revolve around them with constant reference to me, myself and I. They are also poor listeners when it comes to the opinions of others. If they do listen it is with growing impatience, finishing sentences for people and often nodding vigorously in a non-verbal effort to say 'I've heard enough, I get the picture already!'

They seem more concerned with their own qualifications and ever growing CV than they are about their own family, worst of all they rarely recognise they are Type 'A's, appearing blind to their weaknesses and faults. Some are probably born into Type 'A' behaviour whilst others develop the tendencies through upbringing. The traits can be inherited to an extent but beliefs and specific behaviour can be changed, which for these types can have a highly beneficial effect on their productivity, creativity and general health. Ironically, and as hard as they might drive themselves, they rarely reach their desired goals in life; those few that do are never satisfied and always aim for more, with ever-increasing difficulty attached to their goals.

As I said, success does demand that you keep increasing goals and that you keep raising the bar a little. The difference between A's and B's is that the latter keep balanced and are not relying on goals to be happy ('when I get there I'll be happy'), rather they are happy en route.

Recognising these traits is the first step to changing and becoming healthier, happier and more successful.

## Implications to Health for the Type 'A'

This isn't meant to scaremonger, it's just information to help convince those in denial that change is healthy and also that it is never too late to change. The body has a great capacity to heal itself if negative behaviour is exchanged for positive.

The medical fraternity sees Type 'A's as being at risk from high blood pressure, increased cholesterol and coronary heart disease (CHD). A long-term study of Type 'A's (Rosenam et al. 1975. WGGS) involving 3,000 men aged 39–59 taken over an eight and a half year period showed that Type 'A' men were two and a half times more likely to develop CHD (heart disease) as were their Type 'B' counterparts. They were also seen as being twice as likely to suffer from a heart attack.

The Type 'A's already with CHD were five times as likely to have a second heart attack as Type 'B's with the same condition. These finding have been replicated in countries all over the world.

Of all the men in the study two-thirds of those who developed heart disease were Type A, the other third were Type 'B'.

What seems an even more relevant indicator (and predictor) of developing heart disease, more so than type 'A' behaviour, is hostility. Hostile people who are Type 'A' also are highly susceptible to major heart problems.

Type 'B' personalities tend to be very easygoing individuals, very calm about life, unhurried and controlled. They are content with life, not easily irritated or impatient with others and relaxed. Type 'B's are not quick to anger. Faced with traffic jams (or other queues) Type 'B's tend to take the opportunity to have a minute, and are not perturbed about things outside of their control.

Type 'A' personality has been the most extensively researched due to its associated health risks. Other research investigating personality in relation to health behaviours and stress include Temoshok's (1987) study of Type 'C' personality in relation to illness. So let's look at Type 'C' personality.

Type 'C's typically have difficulty expressing their emotions, they lock it all in and tend to suppress or inhibit their feelings, especially those feelings seen as being negative, like anger.

Whilst there is no concrete proof linking Type 'C' personality to illness it does appear, according to the research, to exasperate conditions and influence the progression in those that may already be ill.

## Hardiness

As a contrast to Type 'A' and 'C', other personality types can be protective to the organism (they contribute to good health) in many ways. Hardiness, for example. Hardiness describes individuals with a high sense of personal control over events in their lives and a strong sense of contentment or involvement, together with a tendency to see environmental demands or changes as challenges instead of threats. Hardiness can be developed by exposure therapy – intermittent exposure to the things that make you feel fear (Kobara 1979).

We tend to experience more stress when we feel that something is outside of our control and we can't do anything about it. When it is inside of our control we tend to enjoy it more and see it as a challenge. Often it is only perception (how we view things) that deems something inside or outside of our control.

For instance Julie, an old school friend, was a great swimmer; she loved the demands of swimming even at a highly competitive level. She viewed swimming as fun and successfully competed in many competitions. Although she often competed she did so out of choice, she chose when, and indeed if, she signed up for a competition. It was inside her circle of influence. Subsequently she always enjoyed the challenge and didn't find the overall experience stressful. That is until her perception of competition swimming changed from inside her control to outside. How did this happen? Seeing that she had a lot of potential as a swimmer Julie's teacher started to enter her for more competitions and told her that she had to compete. Now she was planning to compete in most of these contests anyway but by taking away her sense of control the teacher turned the swimming event into a very uncomfortable stressor as opposed to an exciting challenge. Julie became so stressed about forthcoming swimming galas (because she felt she was being forced to enter) that she started to hate swimming and eventually refused to compete.

Perception, if understood, can be changed so that we experience challenge as opposed to fear or stress, but for this to happen we must feel we have at least an element of control and say in our actions.

If you recognise yourself as being part of more than one personality type, don't worry, most people fall into two or three different types. These aren't the only personality types either, there are many more but these are the main ones that have an effect on health, happiness and success. The important thing is to recognise where you are in the whole scope of things and try to turn your weaknesses into strengths. It all starts with self-honesty, which takes intelligence and courage. Later in the book we will look at ways to lessen stress in your life and techniques to change and improve negative perception. For now, please think about the fact that you can change what you are for the better, but only if you are strong enough and perceptive enough to see your weaknesses and do something about them.

# Chapter Seven
# **Immediate Reactions to Stress**

Before we explore the safe release of Rogue Stress Hormones let's first have a look at the common reactions to stress, as brought on by fear, frustration or anxiety. Understanding these reactions helps us to understand ourselves. This is the information age and information is power. You have to appreciate the workings of something if you ever expect to fix it when it breaks down or causes you problems. To be in a position to mend ourselves, with the purpose of living a happier and more fulfilling life, we must first have a profound understanding of how the body works in times of stress, and the unconscious defence mechanisms (cop outs) we employ.

My own quality of life increased dramatically when I first realised that many of my life stresses, created by my own mind, were very natural – something everyone felt – and that I had the ability to change them if I really wanted to. I'm not saying this was an easy task, of course it wasn't, it meant a lot of hard work and re-programming, but it's a lot easier when you at least have the schematics laid out in front of you. In other words, it's easier to find a destination if you have a map.

Briefly, I will go over some of the main reactions, defence mechanisms and coping strategies, we exhibit and employ when fear is imminent. I don't want this to become a book of scholastic mumbo jumbo that only the academic can understand. This book is primarily for the man and woman on the street, to help heal the hurts of what can only be described as a confrontational and often hurtful society.

So how do we react when faced by an uncomfortable stressor, what do we use to shield ourselves from the discomfort of facing stress?

## Aggression

Often one of the first reactions to stress is aggression. Something we all feel at times, though often we are unaware of why. This is usually because most defences to stress occur at an unconscious level. This leaves most of us living in ignorance; forever at the mercy of mood swings and temper tantrums that gain us ill favour with our peers and loved ones.

In my first marriage my biggest frustration was that I didn't know why I was so moody and bad-tempered. If that wasn't bad enough, when the moods did take hold I had no coping strategy to stop them from growing out of control. So a greater portion of my early life was spent either in a mood, in a temper or trying to make amends for the hurt I had inadvertently caused after my emotional outbursts. Because (I felt) I had no control, coupled with my constant over-training, over-thinking and an unhealthy diet I also experienced a lot of depression. I often felt as though these negative emotions could, and would, come and go at their own will, up-turning my life with each visit. I now understand of course that I do have control, but at the time I was not in possession of this information and as a consequence felt violated by life. It wasn't until I realised I could change, I could make a difference, that I started to take control and my life took a turn for the better.

Aggression often manifests itself in an excess of movement, restlessness and tension, unhappiness, involuntary sighing, complaining and procrastination, nail biting and gum chewing, slamming doors and moodiness. These are all physical outlets for stress. Some people drive their excess energy into their work or sport as a positive outlet.

When stress hormones are trapped, looking for a release, the body remains aroused, switched on, ready for action, revving at the traffic lights. It naturally feels an urge to do something physical to release the Rogue Hormones. Basically, the body is looking for its behavioural release, its fight or its flight, its hundred-yard dash to safety, its ten seconds of explosive, defensive aggression, but because most contemporary stressors do not demand this, the physical release does not occur.

If left unattended these strong emotions lead to feelings of anger that have no (conscious) recognisable source. This may also lead to destructive and hostile (displaced) attacks on the people or environment around us.

When we feel angry and act out this aggression, but cannot find any reason for doing so, it becomes a source of stress in itself because the internal parent (what Freud called the superego) punishes us with feelings of guilt and remorse. Also, just the fact that we feel aggressive and angry to those we love, but with no apparent or obvious reason, make us feel as though we have lost the plot, gone crazy, or that we are bad people (this is often compounded when people actually tell us that we are). This feeling becomes yet another stressor on the downward spiral.

I've experienced all of these emotions. I have been so tense due to unutilised stress that the slightest thing in my environment made me feel absolutely enraged. I have even looked at the people closest to me, for very little (often no) provocation, with hate and contempt. Or perhaps they may have made a minor faux pas, which has triggered an aggression in me that was completely out of context.

## The General Adaptation Syndrome

The general adaptation syndrome (GAS) (Selye 1956) is a model that describes how people and animals respond to long-term stress. Selye identified three phases to the general adaptation syndrome, the first of which is the Alarm Stage. This involves the actual fight or flight reactions, which activate the sympathetic division of the ANS (autonomic nervous system). Basically this means that when you feel fear you get adrenalin. If stress continued after the Alarm Stage, once the object that triggered your fear has gone, the body attempts to revert back to normal functioning, whilst at the same time trying to cope with all the extra adrenalin that has been released into the bloodstream, and the subsequent bodily effects this produces. This is Selye's second phase, the Resistance Phase. Following this is Exhaustion (the third phase), which occurs when the body has outstripped its reserves of energy.

The general adaptation syndrome is characterised, in the final phase, by an apparent return to normal levels of heart rate and blood pressure but is identifiable by the very high levels of adrenalin remaining in the bloodstream. Because this excess of adrenalin has not been behaviourally used it produces an immediate and strong – sometimes excessive – reaction to even mild sources of additional stress. In his experiments Selye showed that if an animal is experiencing the general adaptation syndrome, it will show much less resistance to a stress-producing stimulus than an animal that is not in this already aroused condition.

In other words we feel fear, we get adrenalin, the heart rate increases, the blood pressure goes up and the body prepares for a physical encounter. The physical encounter does not happen but we are still full of adrenalin. The body tries to get everything back in balance again by bringing the heart rate and blood pressure back to normal but the body is still aroused, full of adrenalin. Some other, perhaps mild, incident occurs that triggers the fear response and all the adrenalin that was already there is utilised and we find ourselves overreacting to some silly incident.

I remember on one occasion, while busy writing at my computer, asking my wife (who was also busy doing her own jobs) if she would mind making me a cup of tea. Even as I asked her I could feel the aggression building inside me because I was under pressure with a script deadline that had become my stressor. 'Just let me finish this job' she replied (very) reasonably, 'and I'll make you one.'

Now under normal circumstances this would have been fine but because I was full of stress-related adrenalin I stormed out of my chair went into the kitchen and made myself a cup, slamming doors and stamping feet en route. I also distinctly remember mumbling under my breath about 'having to do everything yourself in this bloody house!'

Not very reasonable I know, but something that we all do when the Rogues want their release. Of course I can laugh about it now, I can also stop it from happening because I recognise the signs. And I can quite easily apologise if I do slip up because I know I'm to blame and that Sharon is just a displacement figure.

This is all very important because having the information is one thing; acting on it is quite another. Some of my friends understand about stress and displacement but still don't seem to be able to stop it or apologise to those on the receiving end of their uncontrolled outbursts. Others are still in denial and will not even admit they are victims to the displacement law, or even that they are suffering from denial (they are denying their denial!).

One particular friend, Pete, was facing divorce. He cannot accept that his anger, rage and verbal violence are his responsibility and that his wife is no more than an available displacement figure for the stress incurred in his job. Stringent deadlines have become symbolic tigers and he takes it all out on her. 'It's her fault' he told me vehemently, 'she makes me so angry!'

When I asked him why she was at fault he didn't know. He was unable to define what it was about his wife, other than the fact that she was there, that made her at fault.

The last time I spoke to Pete he asked my advice; what could he do to save his marriage? I advised him to say sorry and take his wife the biggest bunch of roses and the best box of chocolates that he could find and ask for her forgiveness. Then work on finding a better place to use his aggression. Thankfully on this occasion the advice was followed and the marriage saved.

### Step One: Be honest and admit your fault.
### Step Two: Do something about it.

I remember when I first met Sharon. At the time I was working in a very violent and confrontational job, which meant I inadvertently took a lot of my stress home to her. After losing my temper with her one night and smashing a hole in the wall over some triviality, I took her to one side and apologised profusely. I told her, unreservedly, that the problem was mine and I was going to deal with it. I begged her forgiveness and asked her to be patient with me until I found a remedy. This basic communication made a profound difference to us because every time I started to look stressed, Sharon would know what was occurring and not take it all so personally. Some times she'd even tell me off and say 'don't take your stress out on me!' (She can be quite firm sometimes.) Other times she would comfort me and help me through particularly stressful periods, or even suggest that I go for a run to get it out of my system!

It can often be hard to fight the effects of stress on your own. By enlisting the help of those you love you can fight it as a team. Even my children understand displacement because I talk to them about it. We often think that our children are too young to understand and that an apology or explanation is beyond them. Believe me it isn't. They are beautiful little people with feelings and emotions just the same as us, probably even more so. My little lad is only twelve at the time of writing but that doesn't stop me from apologising if I'm a little short with him after a stressful day. I'll say sorry, give him a hug and tell him that I'm cross because I have been very busy and I'm tired. If you make a mistake, erase it with an immediate apology, no matter how hard that might be. It stops stress degeneration dead in its tracks.

## Direct Aggression

Sometimes aggression is expressed directly against the source of frustration, or the stressor, whether that is an individual or an object. Direct aggression sometimes takes the form of a verbal assault, other times a physical assault, both of which are usually countered similarly – you shout at someone, they shout right back, you hit somebody, they hit right back.

Direct aggression is not always hostile or malicious, often it is simply a learned way of problem solving, and in this respect it can be a good thing. However if aggression, direct or otherwise, is inappropriate then it can cause more problems than it solves. It is very much an individual thing, some antagonists will not learn unless you employ direct aggression; others will be horrified and frightened by the very thought of it.

As a doorman I often had to employ direct aggression to neutralise a potential attacker, in this environment with the calibre of people I was dealing with (mostly thick and violent) it was not only appropriate, it was often necessary. Sometimes I was even forced to employ direct physical aggression because that was the only language my antagonists understood, to them a punch in the eye was the usual avenue of discourse.

Unfortunately, to some, physical aggression is a means of communication, often their only means, and if you don't know the speak you can't parley. Having said that, to the greater majority in society any kind of aggression is abhorrent, they see physical aggression as a breaking down of normal communication, so other methods of directing aggression have to be found.

One of my friends, Steve, a nice but very physical man, worked in the media with a lot of middle-class people who were more used to debating across the canteen table than they were fisting it out in the car park. Steve was used to employing direct aggression to make his point in an environment that would tolerate nothing less, but in the world he now found himself this didn't cut the proverbial mustard. Employing direct aggression to make a point with his new work mates did not work. In the short-term he got his own way, but only because he frightened the other staff half to death (secretly they loathed him and thought him a bully). In the long-term it cost him his job because no one would work with him. He wasn't a malicious man; he did not see himself as a bully. Direct aggression was just his way, and in his world it was the norm. When his contract renewal came up for review after the first twelve months he suddenly found himself out of work. What had worked very well in one environment failed abysmally in another.

The irony with people like Steve is, they never seem to learn, and this is as much the fault of those around them as it is their own lack of perception. People become so afraid of direct aggression that they cower to it, their fear turns them into creeping sycophants. So naturally the aggressor thinks that, not only is direct aggression getting results but that people also love them for it, at least to their face.

Beware the ides of March! Behind his back they were plotting his demise because they saw his behaviour as bullying or, at best, antisocial.

In short, sometimes direct aggression works, other times it does not; it is only wisdom that allows us to know when to use it and when not.

Writing to deadlines used to be a major source of stress for me. Writing, generally, can be a stressor anyway because it is such hard work. Sometimes pulling words from my mind is like pulling molars without anaesthetic.

Rather than let my stress overflow into displaced and negative aggression I drive that aggression into other, more positive aspects of my life; my work, my training, my social life.

It's not just self-knowledge that enables me to do this. It's the wisdom gained from having felt it many times before and a history of displacing it positively that makes the difference. It is said that true competence is about growing in wisdom rather than in knowledge, and wisdom only comes from the correct employment of knowledge.

## Displaced Aggression

I know I have already spoken about this in some detail but, as with all aspects of great worth, I think it needs repeating, the more times you hear the same information the more likely it is to stick. For me to really digest something I like to read the same information many times (and often from several different sources). At the moment for instance I have five books on psychology that all offer the same information – written differently by each author. With each reading the information becomes more consolidated and logged in my memory.

Often direct aggression cannot, for whatever reason, be satisfactorily expressed. It may be that the stressor is vague and intangible, the recipient may not even know what the source of stress is because it is often an invisible enemy. Or perhaps the source of stress is very powerful, deeming a direct approach unwise, even dangerous.

If this is the case aggression is usually displaced in an action against an innocent person or object. The college student, who gets bad exam results, takes his aggression out on his room-mate by shouting at him. This is a very basic example. Often the stress builds up and at some point, often days or even weeks after the original stressor, the aggression will come out in a displaced manner. Other times it can be instant, or what I like to call cash displacement. Cash displacement occurs in an almost immediate displacement against something or someone other than the source. A good example is if your wife or husband makes you angry and you punch the wall.

I remember throwing a man out of a pub one night, in my capacity as a doorman, for causing a disturbance. He was very angry with me but didn't have the courage to express his anger directly because I was (he felt) too much of a threat and therefore too dangerous. With no direct outlet available he displaced his anger on the first person that walked past. In this case a young innocent man making his way to the nightclub door. He got battered simply because he was there. This is cash displacement.

People need little justification for this kind of act, but if they want some they usually manufacture it on the spot. In the latter case the man I ejected claimed the youth he attacked was 'screwing him out' and that's why he attacked him.

I also remember another occasion when a doorman from a neighbouring county backed down to a group of local heavies in his nightclub. At the end of the night he was so stressed and embarrassed by the incident, that in a classic display of cash displacement he vented his anger by savagely attacking an innocent passer-by with a baseball bat, leaving him mentally disabled for the rest of his life. The attack on the young student was random and completely unprovoked. To justify, or rationalise his attack the doorman claimed the passer-by was laughing at him. In fact the young student was simply having a joke with his friend after a good night out.

This type of displacement can have catastrophic consequences. The student I just mentioned ended up mentally retarded and in a wheelchair for the rest of his life and the doorman was sentenced to a long jail term.

This kind of negative displacement also has a way of creating a downward spiral of abuse. The boss displaces his stress on his subordinate, who in turn goes home and displaces his aggression on his wife, she shouts at their child who storms into the kitchen and kicks the cat (or worse).

Displacement, when positive and driven, can be a good release for pent-up aggression. Some of the most successful people in the world are successful because they channel (or displace) their aggression positively. When displaced negatively it usually always creates contention and therefore more stress.

This is displacement on a small scale, though it can have life-changing consequences.

Steve – just one example of many – lost his wife and beautiful children because of negative displacement. He was not unlike many other people in that he had a lot of stress in his life, which derived from his job, where he had to shoulder a lot of responsibility. But his displacement cost him his liberty, and as a direct result, his family.

It was the weekend and Steve nipped out in the car to get a video for the kids. He'd had a busy and stressful week at work and was looking forward to spending the weekend relaxing with his family. On his way to the video shop another car accidentally cut him up. Nothing unusual in that, just a common everyday event. But Steve was so incensed, and so angry he got out of the car and argued with the other driver. The argument became heated and, after a little pushing and shoving, Steve lashed out. It took four people to pull him off the hapless driver. The police and ambulance were on the scene in moments and Steve was whisked straight off to the cells, remanded (the police were having a purge on road rage at the time) and later given a custodial sentence, which is where he is right now. He still hasn't got back home to see his children. He has lost his job and his home. And his wife is now on Valium due to the stress. All due to negative displacement and a moment of spontaneous weakness.

Interestingly, it could also be said that the courts are guilty of similar displacement, or scapegoating.

Matty, a very good friend of mine, was recently sentenced to a jail term of twelve months on a charge that deserved no more than a fine. Matty and some friends went to an out-of-town club to celebrate his twenty-first birthday. As they were leaving the club at the end of the night a fight started with some local youths. Matty and his friends got pulled into the affray more out of bad luck than anything else. No one was badly hurt, it was just a scuffle really, but the police became involved and all the lads were charged with a public disorder offence. They were all told by their solicitors to expect a fine, at the very most.

Four out of the six lads had good jobs and none had any previous convictions. As bad luck would have it their case came to court at the same time as reports of football violence were being heavily reported in the media (France during the World Cup). Every newspaper seemed to be running front-page reports on the violence. In court, at the end of the case, the judge's summing up heavily reflected the tabloid reports. In a classic display of displacement the judge told the lads, 'I am not interested in your backgrounds or excuses, I am sure that is exactly what the football hooligans are saying in France right now. I am giving you all a custodial sentence.'

## Societal Displacement

Prejudice and violence against minority groups is often linked to scapegoating or displacement. In the old American Deep South it was recorded that violence against black people rose substantially when the price of cotton was low, and the lower the price fell the greater the violence grew. Similarly, in England, there used to be a lot of racist attacks against Indian people when unemployment for whites was high.

Violence in society is often a manifestation of economic frustration, when people are out of work and money is scarce, societal violence is exasperated.

## Apathy

At the opposite end of the scale to active aggression lies apathy, indifference and withdrawal. It is unknown why people react in different ways to stress and tension, though it is thought it might be a learned response from childhood, much the same as any other behaviour.

This kind of response is characterised by people who lead apathetic lifestyles and settle for second best. Many people are unhappy with their lot but seem at a loss to anything about it. They are often employed in jobs that do not fulfil them, they drive cars they don't want to drive and live in houses they would rather not live in – often with partners that they no longer love. In short they are living lives they feel could be so much more rewarding. Rather than do anything about it they seem to fall into this apathetic state where they feel that, no matter what they do, it will not make a difference.

## Learned Helplessness

Another type of apathy is known as learned helplessness. Have you ever heard the story of the elephant and the twig? (I have a book out by the same name). In India they train obedience in elephants (to stop them from escaping) by tying them to a huge tree when they are still very young. The tree is so large that no matter how hard the baby elephant pulls and tugs it cannot escape. As the elephant gets bigger the tree they are tied to gets smaller until, as a fully-grown adult, they can be tied to a twig and they won't escape, in fact they won't even try.

The Elephant and The Twig.

The early training using the large tree develops learned helplessness in the elephant. After trying so hard and for so long to escape, only to be thwarted time and again, it eventually believes that, no matter what it does, it cannot escape. When, ultimately, it is tied only to a twig it doesn't even bother to try.

People are similar; if they are told often enough that they cannot escape mediocrity, that they cannot achieve, that they cannot escape, eventually that belief will become so strong, so real, they, like the elephant, won't even bother to try.

As a young man dreaming of becoming a writer I was always told by my peers, and more specifically by my first wife, that 'people like us don't write books'. Comments such as 'don't get above your station', 'be happy with what you've already got', and, 'why can't you be satisfied with the factory like everyone else?' were the staple diet fed to me by my peers.

Every time I tried to get out of my environment and better myself I would be reprimanded for being (in their words) pretentious. In the end I believed what I had been told so much I stopped trying. In fact I got so bad that even thinking about a career in writing made me feel depressed, worthless, apathetic and withdrawn because I, like the elephant, believed there was no escape. Only when I broke the grip of those around me by questioning their truth was I able to sever the tie and achieve success.

I was only being held back by a twig, though until I pulled really hard it felt like an oak tree.

Friends can be metaphoric oaks also. Later when I had achieved a measure of success one of my closest friends constantly tried to pull me down and unfairly criticise my success. Either he was very jealous, very insecure or maybe a bit of both. Whatever the reason he would verbally attack me at any given chance to make me feel bad about escaping, to the point where I started to avoid him. When I did pull away he projected the blame and said to friends 'I don't see Geoff any more, he's not interested now that he's made it'.

It has also been reported that prisoners of war often become apathetic when constantly faced with the threat of deprivation, torture and death. The more severe cases resulted in death, the recipients giving up on life believing they were (they felt) powerless to make a difference.

In scenarios such as this there are two remedies which pull people from their stupor and stop the downward spiral. One is getting them to their feet and making them do something, no matter how trivial. The second remedy is getting them involved with the salvation or redemption of other prisoners or some current or future problem. This often helps to snap them out of their apathy.

Left to its own devices, apathy can quickly lead into depression, breakdowns and even suicide. What was learned from this, and subsequently put into practice in later conflicts, was that the prisoners need to retain some sense of purpose, they need to follow a schedule of regular routines; like rising at a certain time in the morning, maintaining their own personal hygiene and training regularly. Basically it was seen as imperative that they keep busy and organised. As Blake so succinctly put it, 'a busy bee has no time for sorrow'. These occupying endeavours exercised the will of the prisoners so that it did not, could not, and would not atrophy. It's the same as most things in life; if you don't use it you lose it.

## Fantasy

Many people use fantasy to escape their stress. When their world becomes gloomy they escape to a fantasyland, an idyllic place somewhere in their own imagination. These Walter Mitty types cannot face life head on because their world never seems to be the way they want it to be. Of course we all share the same world and how we see it is simply a matter of perception. The pessimist will tell you that his glass is half empty because that's how he views the world, the optimist on the other hand will tell you that his glass is half full because he sees what he has got and not what he hasn't.

It's like the lovely little poem about the two chaps in jail, 'two men look through prison bars, one sees mud the other stars'.

Fantasising is not all bad; it can be a form of positive visualisation where, in the mind's eye, we see our dreams. When I was an up-and-coming writer (before I published my first book) I always used to imagine how great it might feel to be a published writer (or a 'real' writer as I used to think of it). It was my dream, and fantasising became an exercise in visualisation, which to me at that time was a good thing. It starts becoming negative and non-productive when you don't actually do anything other that fantasise. There needs to be a strong work ethic to make your dreams a reality otherwise it is energy wasted. Some people sit up all night dreaming about it, others stay up all night doing it.

I don't think fantasy, as a temporary respite, is harmful; it can even be a beneficial way of giving your head a rest from the stress. But if you use it too often there is a very real danger you might end up with your head in the clouds and do nothing else but dream. Subsequently, when you're brought back to reality by the boom of the foreman's voice telling you to 'get back to the broom' it can be very depressing. Also, for the extremists in society (you know who you are, you blighters), there is the danger of actually becoming Walter Mitty and losing the ability to distinguish between reality and fantasy. Coupled with hard work and determination fantasising, I believe, is a good thing. On its own it is wasted energy and can lead to greater apathy and depression.

Perhaps equally as worrying are those individuals who get so disillusioned by life that they refuse to use fantasy at all.

Julian and his wife used to drive out in the country to look at the posh houses and fantasise about the day when they might own one themselves. It used to be a Sunday treat for them. Later they stopped doing it because, as Julian said 'there's no use in dreaming about something you're never going to get, you just set yourself up for disappointment'.

When Julian said this I felt very sad for him. I knew he had given up the ghost, he had thrown in the towel.

I believe with all of my heart we can have anything we want from life, anything. We just have to work hard for it and believe, and we will get it. If you don't believe then of course it is unlikely to happen. Thus far life has given me everything I have asked for, and I believe it will grant all my future wishes too. We are creators, we can create, and we can have our greatest desires. We have the ability to do this. I have been at the very bottom of the pile and I have mixed with those at the very top and let me tell you that there is nothing separating those at the bottom and those at the top other than belief and a strong work ethic.

There is a lot of responsibility that comes with being able to create, once we accept this gift we can no longer blame anybody else if things do not go to plan. It's down to us. People love having someone to blame for their unhappiness, be it the tax man, the wife, the mother-in-law, the weather, the country, the unions, God, whatever, there is always someone to blame if you look hard enough. When you latch on to the greatest secret of mankind, that we are the creators, the buck stops with us and there is no one to blame but ourselves.

People only do what we allow them to do. My school bully only intimidated me because I allowed him to do so, and although I spent a long time blaming him for my problems it was really my own fault because I allowed it to happen. Similarly I blamed my ex-wife for keeping me stuck in the factory for nine years. She was my excuse for not leaving. 'If it wasn't for her', I told everyone that would listen, 'I'd be out of here in a heartbeat'. She was a convenient scapegoat, and although she did hold me back it was only because I let her. In fact I was glad for the excuse because it meant that I didn't have to get out there and take risks. I used to have an awful job in a chemical factory, I hated it. But, I couldn't leave. My wife wouldn't let me. That's what I kidded myself.

One day she turned around and said that if I was really that unhappy I should leave the factory and find a job that I did like. Well, I nearly fell over. I was scared half to death. Now I had no one to blame but myself; the realisation hit me like a hammer. It was hard to look myself in the mirror for a while I can tell you. And when I did look I didn't see the brave, hard-done-to guy that I had seen before. I saw a weak and insecure young man who had survived a confrontational existence on Freudian defence mechanisms.

Our environment or our influences often trigger apathy but ultimately it only occurs if we let it. We have a potentially indomitable spirit if we will it.

## Anxiety

Any situation that threatens our well-being or the well-being of the organism is, in psychological terms, assumed to produce what we know as the state of anxiety. Conflicts or objects that block our path to a desired goal are one form of anxiety. Another common form, one that I think we can all associate with, is that of physical harm. Threats to self-esteem or pressure to perform beyond ones capacities are others.

Anxiety is a worry, apprehension, dread or fear that we all experience in varying degrees.

Freud spoke of the importance of anxiety but differentiated between Objective Anxiety and Neurotic Anxiety. (Just in case you are interested he believed that Neurotic Anxiety was the result of an unconscious conflict between id impulses – mainly sexual and aggressive – and the constraints imposed by the ego or superego, usually because this conflicted with personal or moral values).

Objective Anxiety is a realistic response to a perceived threat in the environment, like the threat of attack or the threat of physical danger (a mugger in an entry), is synonymous with fear.

Neurotic Anxiety, he believed, stemmed from an unconscious conflict; problems that we have pushed to the backs of our minds that keep trying to re-surface.

A distinction between the two helps, it's meaningful but it is still unclear that the two emotions can be differentiated either on the basis of physiological responses or the individual's description of the feeling. That is, although Objective and Neurotic Anxiety are different and might occur for very different reasons, the chemicals released and the feelings felt are the same. So whether it is a mugger in an entry (an objective threat) or something in our mind (an imagined threat), the brain sees them both as a sabre-toothed tiger, and so responds with physiological fight or flight (adrenalin) to prepare us for the expected conflict.

So the terms 'fear' and 'anxiety' are often seen as synonymous (they feel the same) and interchangeable, therefore when we talk about fear we also mean anxiety and when we say anxiety we also mean fear, they are as one. Phew! Time for a cup of tea.

## Physical Reactions to Stress

Let's have a look at the bodily reactions to stress and why adrenalin is released. Understanding the physical manifestations of stress is very important. Most people wrongly associate these reactions with cowardice, which does nothing at all to enhance self-esteem. For instance, trembling limbs are a natural by-product of the adrenal release, but how many times have you heard the comment, 'he was so scared he was shaking like a leaf!' This is said with derogatory undertones implying cowardice or weakness. We even put ourselves down due to our ignorance; 'I don't know what's the matter with me, I'm shaking like a baby!'

If we associate these bodily reactions with fear and cowardice it creates self-doubt, which is a precursor to throwing in the towel. So it is important that we recognise the natural and expected reactions and learn to deal with them in a positive way.

We also have a moral dilemma in this paradoxical society where both fight and flight are unacceptable to the general populace. If we employ direct aggression at the source of our anxiety (especially if it's physical) we are often seen by our peers as antisocial, even thugs; if however we listen to natural instinct and run away from confrontation we're branded as cowards. People who do not face up to their problems are often looked upon as weak. Because of this moral dilemma the adrenal syndrome has become an antiquated commodity and as a consequence instinct is cupboarded. Also the natural bodily reactions associated with fight or flight are so misunderstood they are now seen as signs of weakness, or even misinterpreted as signs of illness.

As I have already said, and forgive me for labouring the point, the brain cannot distinguish between differing forms of confrontation and so releases adrenalin, carte blanche, for most forms of confrontation (real or neurotic). Actors freeze on stage (stage fright) because of anticipation or over-anticipation. Children go blank on exam day because blood is drawn away from non-vital areas of the body (those seen as non-vital in fight or flight), one of these being the brain, inducing memory loss or distortion. Because fight or flight can cause memory loss and memory distortion (and the worry of exams causes the stress release) we really do our children a disservice when we make them sit pressure-exams and we definitely do not see them at their best. If the onus were placed perhaps on continual, ongoing coursework, as opposed to set exams on a set date we would decrease their stress and enhance their knowledge. The idea of learning is to increase and stimulate brain activity. With contemporary research into stress and its effects on the brain strongly suggesting that unutilised cortisol (a chemical released during stress) actually aids in the destruction of brain cells, we hardly want to do that.

Coming back to my original point; I think we'd all probably agree that it's sensible to run away from a violent encounter, it's survival. It might not be the right choice to run away from an intangible confrontation however, because most problems have to be met and overcome at some point.

If we misread the signs and allow confusion to enter the equation we may well find ourselves frozen with fear and unable to function clearly in our work or in our life.

With this in mind I will list the common reactions to fear to enable you to recognise normal bodily reactions. It stops the downward spiral and allows you to deal with the anxiety roadblock, which is jamming your thoroughfare.

Before we look at the bodily reactions, let's firstly look at the adrenal map, and the different types of adrenal release.

## The Fear of Fear Itself

Often you may not know why you feel fear and so you look for the reason or the logic behind your anticipation. Basically, if you can pinpoint your fear it can help you to better deal with it. If you can't find a reason, there probably isn't one, other than natural anticipation. We all feel it in confrontation. So don't bother trying to look for logic where there is none, it'll just add confusion and tiredness to discomfort.

Confusion creates internal conflict; this overworks the brain resulting in huge energy loss, indecision and self-doubt, which in turn can cause capitulation or withdrawal.

My daughter would spend weeks building up to school exams (oh, if only I knew then what I know now!). She always experienced adrenal release that caused her a lot of discomfort. She got so bad that she often felt like giving up and not doing the exams. She'd spend hours trying to analyse why she felt so scared but could never find a reason. The concentration made her very tired and mentally weak because, although the brain only weighs two per cent of our body weight it can, in times of worry and concentration, use up to 50 per cent of our oxygen. That's why a champion chess player may lose 7lb in weight over one week of tournaments.

There was no tangible reason for my daughter's fear other than natural anticipation; her brain saw the exams as a sabre-toothed tiger. I told her why she was feeling scared and that she should channel her energies into her study for the forthcoming exam (positive displacement). Suffice to say she passed with flying colours, but it was only because I put a name to her woes. Once she understood what was happening it no longer had a hold over her.

If there is no reason don't try and look for one, if you do you'll be wasting valuable energy that could be better employed.

## Anticipatory Adrenalin

This occurs with things like anticipation of having to talk in public, an exam, a big sales meeting, a forthcoming karate competition, a planned confrontation with the husband, wife, neighbour or boss. The list is endless.

When you anticipate confrontation you may experience slow releases of adrenalin, often even months before a planned confrontation. Due to the longevity of anticipatory release, it can wear and corrode the recipient both mentally and physically.

If my confrontation is not for another week then I don't really need performance enhancing adrenalin until closer to the time. If I have to talk in public next Saturday, and today is Monday, I do not need fight or flight for another four days. So for four days I am getting adrenalin that I do not want or need. In a week of anticipation the adrenal release is going to take away my appetite, my sleep, in fact my life may go on hold until the confrontation is over. I am sure we have all experienced this.

During the week of anticipation I'm likely to be like a bear with a sore head and hell to live with. This is why so many doormen, police and stressed businessmen end up in the divorce courts, their spouses cannot live with the mood swings and the impatience.

If you have a week until the confrontation, but are getting daily releases of adrenalin, release the adrenalin on a daily basis, a kind of psychological de-sludge if you like. Have a long hard run, hit the bag, swing a golf club, go for a swim or a dance (this is a Safe Surrogate Release). Get it out of your system. Once utilised your appetite will return and sleep will be easier.

I missed out on so many things when I was younger due to anticipatory adrenalin. As soon as the feelings of fear started I felt like a coward. This in turn caused me to doubt myself and, before I knew it, I'd lost the will to continue. I'd make some lame excuse as to why I couldn't do whatever it was I was meant to do, then withdraw as quietly as possible. Of course, when you've backed down once it becomes easier and easier to back down the next time and the next until, all of a sudden, you have a long history of failures behind you. Over a long period anticipatory adrenalin is a metaphoric monkey on your back and this monkey has a habit of getting fat.

## Anticipation of Consequence

When you anticipate consequence before a confrontation even begins, the fear of that consequence, whatever it might be, often encourages you to abort. The best way to deal with fear of consequence is – and this always works for me – accept the consequences beforehand. Look at the worst case scenario and say to yourself, 'yeah, if that happens I can handle it.' Then set about making plans to improve on the worst that can happen. Once you have accepted the worst case scenario the fear of it can no longer intimidate you.

## Adrenal Dump

This generally occurs when anticipation is not present, or a situation escalates unexpectedly fast, or the recipient feels completely out of their depth. The feeling of adrenal dump is often so intense that the recipient freezes in the face of confrontation, the reasoning process mistaking it for sheer terror (if the confrontation is a life-threatening one it might well be sheer terror). Adrenal dump is the most devastating of all adrenal releases.

It often occurs when a confrontation arises that you were not ready or prepared for, usually the same scenarios as those that cause slow release but with no prior notice.

When I interviewed a group of soldiers for my book *Fear – The Friend of Exceptional People* they all said they had never experienced adrenal dump. This was probably because they were all constantly in anticipation of confrontation, and when anticipation is present there can be little chance of dump.

Due to the fact that most people in society are switched off to the realities of what is happening around them ('it will never happen to me') most confrontational moments will be unexpected and therefore cause adrenal dump. Avoidance comes from being constantly aware of your surroundings and being aware of your bodily reactions to confrontation. If you are switched off on either count, adrenal dump is the likely consequence.

## Secondary Adrenalin

Before, during or after a confrontation, unexpected occurrences, things that you hadn't planned for, can (and do) cause a secondary kick of adrenalin. The brain, sensing your lack of preparedness, sees it as a physical threat to the organism and releases a secondary injection of adrenalin that is nearly always mistaken for fear. It tends to happen when you think that a situation is resolved and instead of retaining a degree of awareness you go into a celebratory state. When the situation suddenly re-emerges you get an unexpected kick of adrenalin that forces you to freeze (or run) or certainly feel tremendous anticipation. If you think a situation is over and you drop your guard you will be wide open to secondary adrenalin. That's why the Samurai of old always said 'after the battle is over tighten your helmet straps.'

My advice is, no matter how resolved you think the situation is, retain your awareness. It's like the story of the guy who got attacked by a mugger and beat the mugger up, he was so pleased with him self that he dropped his awareness, after all, no one gets mugged twice in one night! He did. He was so surprised by the second attack that he completely froze and his courage left him, the mugger ran off with his belongings and he didn't even put up a fight. Expect the unexpected and you'll never be taken by surprise.

## Peripheral Adrenalin

Often people are aware, or they think that they are, but their awareness is tunnelled. That is, they are so indoctrinated into expecting a confrontation to fit a certain place or type (or a situation to unfold in a certain manner) that they are completely taken by surprise when it occurs outside the periphery of their expectations. Awareness needs to be 360 degrees.

What also happens a lot in reality is we get 'pincered' by wily antagonists (or competitors) whilst our awareness is tunnelled. The best way to manage this syndrome is to keep your awareness holistic.

## Anticipation of Consequence (during a confrontation)

I have seen many fall foul of this syndrome, giving up in the midst of a confrontation because they suddenly think about (or are deliberately or inadvertently reminded of) the consequences of their actions. This often occurs at a crisis point within the conflict, when things are not going according to plan. Thinking about the possible consequences of your actions (again success, failure or retribution) triggers adrenalin. If this is mistaken for fear it often leads to capitulation.

It happens quite a lot in business when people suddenly feel as though they are out of their depth, or, if they are facing a wily or malicious adversary they might be told they are out of their depth to force capitulation. I remember the time that I was working at a factory on shifts, a job I hated with a vengeance. I had been trying to get off shifts for quite a while and I moaned about my predicament to the manager of the factory and to my wife and probably to anyone else that would listen (in my defence I was very young). Eventually I was offered a move to a lovely little job on the day shift, a drop in money but a nice little number away from the depressive shift work that I had endured for five years. I was all set to move, the plans were made and I only had about a week left of the shift work. Suddenly I found myself thinking deeply about the consequences of the move. What if I absolutely hated the new job; I mean I didn't like the one I had but better the devil you know and all that. What if I didn't get on with my new work mates? I'd hate to be stuck for eight hours a day with people I didn't like. And the wages! The drop was quite substantial, would I manage? What if, when I got to the new job, the work fell short and they started having redundancies? I'd be the last in and subsequently the first out. I overanticipated all the possible negative consequences, all things that were very unlikely to happen but could happen, and I literally scared myself out of moving to a much better job. I went to see my manager and asked him could I stay, I had changed my mind. I made lots of excuses about why I wanted to stay but the bottom line was that I lost my nerve because of overanticipation.

## Post-fight Anticipation

After confrontation, whether successful or not, the body often secretes slow releases of adrenalin. This is brought on when confrontation is so difficult that it forces the body and mind into overload leaving the recipient mentally and physically drained. This overload often becomes its own stressor triggering the release of stress hormones. Like the lobster that labours to shed its shell so that it might grow. When the shell is finally shed he is so weak that he cannot defend himself against prey. Be aware that when confrontation (or growth) is over you will be temporarily impaired, a little weaker than normal. This is only until you grow a new shell, but until then you are vulnerable so be on your guard, tighten your helmet straps.

It can also be brought on by post-fight anticipation, when we over anticipate the consequences of our actions.

I remember as a young man being selected to fight in the national Gung-Fu squad for the system that I represented. I had fought well in the association championships to get my place and after the fight when I was offered a place on the squad, I was delighted. That is until my post-fight fear of consequence set in. I knew I was physically capable of fighting at that level but the thought of fighting at that level *permanently* scared the hell out of me. With my promotion to squad member I would have to take on the added pressure of *being* a squad member, part of which was upping my training and travelling to all of the competitions where I would have to face some of the best fighters in the country. I had achieved what I had set out to do but after the fight I doubted my ability to handle it now I was there. And so, of course, due to my limiting belief in myself I didn't handle it. I told friends I wasn't scared, I just didn't want to do it, I told them that I had 'gone off competition.' I (like my friend in the earlier story) even blamed them for placing too much emphasis on competition. The bottom line was: I bottled it. But really, I suppose, looking at it objectively with the information I have in front of me now, I didn't bottle it, I just got tricked by my survival instinct to run away from what it perceived as a life-threatening event. In fact, I would go as far as to say that no one really bottles it; we are all just tricked. At that time in my life my survival instincts were a lot stronger than my will or my knowledge.

For the record I came to terms with this syndrome later in my life when I learned to understand myself and my reactions to confrontation. I eventually fought in many competitions, even on an international level, when I travelled to America to fight against the USA national squad.

I had another friend who was a very talented writer and had always wanted his own column in the magazine of which I am sub-editor. His work was of a high standard and he had some great ideas, so I put the proposal to my editor, who readily agreed to give my friend the chance he was looking for. He was offered his own column, which is a sure-fire way to high profile and a good income. Once he had the column post-confrontation anticipation he knocked on the door. What if his writing wasn't up to the standard? What if people didn't like the content of his articles? What if he didn't know as much about his subject matter as he thought he knew and tripped himself up professionally? What if someone took offence to his writing and threatened him (it happens in the martial arts!)? His mind was full of 'what ifs' and all he could think about were the dire consequences. My friend talked himself out of his dream job by frightening himself half to death with the worry of the consequences. Of course there is always the possibility of things going wrong as there is a consequence to all the things that we do in life, but the majority of these fears are completely unfounded. They say that 95 per cent of the things that we fear never happen. Of the five per cent left, tell yourself that if they happen 'you'll handle it' because you always will.

## Stress Conglomeration

Those who work or live in a stress-filled environment or those simply suffering from long-term stress may experience a conglomeration of all the releases. Slow release, because they constantly anticipate confrontation; adrenal dump when situations unexpectedly occur in their environment; and aftermath as a consequence of their confrontation. At once the recipient may experience a concoction of all adrenal releases and, if not checked, this can have an upsetting and detrimental effect on their health and personal life.

## What to Do

The most important thing is to recognise what is happening to your body. Explain to the people in your life how and why you feel so they do not simply see you as impossible to live with. Release your stress physically on a regular basis with a Safe Surrogate Release. If it all gets too much pull away from the arena and give yourself a good rest, mentally and physically.

In confrontational moments, when adrenalin is released, the recipient may experience physical reactions. These reactions might need to be hidden from your competitors;

if not hidden they allow competitors to manipulate and play on them. This is done with the Duck Syndrome.

## The Duck Syndrome

Hiding the physical reactions to fear is a technique I call the Duck Syndrome. If you watch a duck in a pond it will glide gracefully through the water with very little outward movement. It takes on a look of ease. However, under the water, where you can't see, his little webbed feet will be going like the clappers. Similarly we should learn to hide the reactions to the adrenal syndrome by controlling the bodily reactions to adrenalin, showing no signs of the way we feel inside. This way the opponent cannot get a measure of your emotional state. Very often if they perceive you as being fearless, because you are employing the Duck Syndrome, they may capitulate. When ignorance is mutual, confidence is king.

These are some of the immediate and expected bodily reactions to adrenalin. In a later chapter we will look at the expected and recognised bodily effects of short-term and long-term stress, as opposed to immediate reactions to it.

## Pre-fight Shakes

Your legs, and possibly other limbs, may shake uncontrollably. In fight or flight blood is taken from the non-vital areas of the body and pumped to those that are seen as essential for a physical response (running or fighting). This causes the major limbs, especially the legs, to shake. It's a little like a car sat at the traffic lights with its engine revving, waiting for the green light. Your body is revving, waiting for action. I control leg shaking by tapping the heel of one foot, as though tapping to the beat of an imaginary song. This conscious leg tapping gives the effect of an unperturbed person who is not scared.

## Dry Mouth

Your mouth may become dry and pasty as the throat opens to allow more oxygen to the lungs. It can be uncomfortable and inhibit speech. Whenever I talk in public I like to have a drink of water close by to counteract this dryness because it can affect the pitch of the voice, which is not good when you are trying to appear confident.

## Voice Quiver

Your voice may acquire a nervous and audible tremor. This is a bad one. It is hard to sound confident when your vocal cords are doing an involuntary bossa nova. A quivery voice says to anyone, in any language, that you are scared.

Many people actually become monosyllabic, that is, they cannot speak coherently or they fall into single syllables, very short sentences, or they cannot talk at all.

In days of old, when men roamed with woolly mammoths, articulate speech was an absolutely non-vital commodity in fight or flight. With today's opponent the voice is a vital commodity. An actor feeling the effects of 'stage fright' is not much good without his voice. A businessman needs the use of his voice in meetings; a politician would be an ineffective campaigner without his voice, or if his voice was all of a quiver.

The best way to learn voice control in confrontational moments is to step into any arena that brings on adrenalin such as the boxing ring, public speaking or teaching venues and practise. Learn to control the quiver and hide the effects of fear. Diaphragmatic breathing (breathing deeply in through the nose and filling the belly, as opposed to the chest) is a great help as it slows down the adrenalin and brings calm, allowing more control of the voice.

## Tunnel Vision

On the positive side, tunnel vision enhances visual concentration. Its negative by-product is blinkering of peripheral vision. Background and bystanders are often lost to cortical perception. The tangible source of your fear (if there is one) appears closer and larger due to the optical illusion caused by the effect. To widen the peripheral field it is wise to step back a little (if this is possible).

What I also find effective, if appropriate, is to swill your face with very cold water. One of my friends told me that, when entering the boxing ring, his trainer used to place ice on the back of his neck which, he says, used to bring back full vision.

## Perspiration

The palms of the hands often sweat profusely. In fact you tend to sweat all over the body. Soldiers patrolling in volatile areas like Northern Ireland will often sweat away 7lb in body weight in four or five hours of patrolling due to fearful anticipation. Sweat acts as a coolant to the working muscles preparing for a physical encounter.

## Nausea

Stress may cause vomiting, or the feeling of wanting to vomit. Undigested food is seen as excess baggage in fight or flight so the body will try to throw it up to make you lighter and more efficient.

## Relaxed Bowels or Bladder

The recipient may experience temporary weakening of bowel or bladder control. Again, digested food and drink is also seen as non-vital to fight or flight so will be discarded. In the nightclub, working as a doorman, it was not uncommon to see the toilet full of doormen, emptying their bladders, prior to an expected fight. And in a karate or full contact competition the toilets will also be full of competitors getting rid of 'excess baggage'. It is common and natural. However it is not always socially acceptable in this society to urinate or defecate on the confrontational periphery, so we have learned to control the instinct. Before big meetings businessmen often find themselves constantly wanting to urinate or defecate. People with long-term stress react similarly.

## Adrenal Deafness (Auditory Exclusion)

Sometimes, when the threat becomes so overwhelming that concentration is greatly enhanced, peripheral noise, even as loud as a scream or gunshot are completely cut out and not recognised by the recipient.

## Fugue State

Adrenal exposure, particularly adrenal dump, can cause anatomic, even robotic verbal response. Sometimes these responses are not remembered after the event. This is partly due to the memory loss or distortion associated with dump. Sometimes terrifying aspects of a confrontation may be completely blocked out and yet, paradoxically, trivial things loom large in recall. Also, the sequence of events or words may also be altered or lost in the memory.

## The Black and White (Amaurosis Fugax)

Due to the amount of blood drawn from the brain in fight or flight the recipient often sees whole situations in black and white, all colour disappears, as though they are watching a black and white TV.

## Total Acquiescence

If misunderstood or not controlled the adrenal syndrome, certainly adrenal dump, can evoke feelings of helplessness and abject terror, often bringing on extreme feelings of depression and foreboding. Tears and often hysteria may also occur.

## Astral Experience (Excorporation)

In extreme cases the recipient of the adrenal syndrome experiences an out of body experience, feeling as though they are outside of themselves watching the action spectator-like.

## Logorrhea

It is very common for the recipient to experience (post-confrontation) the compulsion to verbally justify their actions with non-stop and very fast speech.

## Denial Response

In extreme circumstances, serious physical attack, etc., the recipient can be temporarily psychologically unable or unwilling to accept responsibility for their actions, 'I didn't stab him, he ran on to the knife! It wasn't my fault.'

## Time Distortion or Loss and Memory Distortion or Loss (Tachypsychia)

Many people have reported that a stressful moment seemed to last an eternity, when in reality it may have only lasted a few minutes or even seconds. During confrontation, time can appear to stand still, one minute often feeling like one hour. Paradoxically others have said, 'It all happened so fast'.

After confrontation, memories of the event can become distorted ('My attacker was seven feet tall and seventeen stone.' In fact he was only five foot eleven and fourteen stone), or even lost. Sometimes, after an elapsed period of time, the memories might gradually come back, though sometimes they never return.

## Death by Fright

In a tiny minority of cases some have been known to die from fright. According to an article in *New Scientist* magazine, the terrorised brain (terrorised by fear or severe stress) of a healthy person triggers the release of a mix of chemicals so potent that it induces a cataclysmic influx of calcium into the heart cells. This causes the heart to contract so fiercely that it never relaxes again. Heart cells have a channel that lets calcium in, which is regulated by what are known as catecholamines. When nerves release catecholamines directly into the heart, these channels open like floodgates and the cells fill with calcium, triggering the contraction of the muscle fibres. The theory is that a severe fright sometimes makes nerves release massive amounts of catecholamines. This causes so much calcium to go into the fibres that they seize up completely. 'The heart', *New Scientist* says, ' has contracted like a focal rigor mortis, it has turned to stone in seconds'. Death is almost instantaneous as the muscle damage sends the heart into a chaotic arrhythmia.

All of the forgoing feelings are usual (bar the last which is extremely rare); recognise and accept them, they are part and parcel of the stress response and, although unpleasant, quite natural. These reactions do lessen in intensity, as you become more familiar with them and as you learn coping strategies. Many mistake these natural reactions as either illness ('there must be something wrong with me I can't stop going to the toilet!') or cowardice ('I was so scared I nearly wet my pants!'). In most cases they are neither, rather they are the expected reactions to what is a very physical response.

Failure to recognise this will cause self-doubt and possibly, capitulation.

The more you can learn and understand about the immediate effects of stress, the easier it becomes to lessen the intensity of (or lose completely) these reactions.

## Chapter Eight
# Symptoms of Short-term and Long-term Stress

Some of the following list may not relate directly to how you are feeling right now, but I do know from experience that these lists offer solace to those who are suffering from stress – short or long-term. Even if it only adds validity to the benign nature of their symptoms it reduces stress because worrying about symptoms is, in itself, a stressor. Again, it is about putting names to problems so that we can gain power over them. Please note that I am not a doctor. If you have health worries please seek medical help. This is just a general guide.

First let us look at some of the behavioural symptoms of stress.

## Increased Cigarette Smoking

People use cigarettes to ease their stress but smoking can cause anxiety because of its expensive and very unhealthy nature. Nicotine also restricts blood flow to the brain which can be a cause of stress in itself. It's common for people under stress to reach for the cigarettes and it may relax them in the short-term, but it is a suppressant and not a cure, in the long-term it kills millions of people.

## Over-eating and Obesity

Many stressed people automatically reach for the biscuit barrel. They comfort-eat. As a result they often pile on the pounds. In a society that sees slim-as-in, weight gain is a stressor in its own right because it affects the way we see ourselves; and the way we think others see us. This has a detrimental effect on our self-esteem. Also, by the very nature of binge eating we tend to crave all the wrong food types, particularly sugar and salts.

## Sugar

We tend to crave sugar because, in fight or flight, the primary source of fuel is glucose. To give us that extra energy (or even to replace the glucose that has already been used) we crave something sweet (sucrose, maltose, glucose, fructose, dextrose and lactose are all sugars) in the form of sweets or foods that are high in sugar content.

As previously stated, if the stressor does not find a physical release the extra sugar is a hindrance and not a help. This extra sugar acts as a catalyst for adrenalin (it stimulates the adrenal gland to release adrenalin), which exasperates the problem more. So, if possible, sugary foods should be kept to a minimum in times of stress.

## Salt

Too much salt is not good either. In large quantities salt affects blood pressure and, therefore triggers the stress response.

## Loss of Appetite and Anorexia

Paradoxically, others lose their appetite in times of stress and fail to eat adequately. During flight or fight appetite is often suppressed and the digestive tracts temporarily close down. We go from metabolic metabolism (which is our normal metabolism where bodily functions, digestion, cell repairs, etc., are constantly being undertaken) to the emergency catabolic metabolism (where all normal functions are either suppressed or placed on maintenance). In catabolic metabolism all energy is directed towards those areas of the body that are seen as vital for a physical response. This is why the appetite is suppressed and as a result weight is, or can be affected. This can and often does become a stressor in itself because we often associate weight loss with ill health. The more weight we lose the more stressed we become. It is a downward spiral to very ill health, often anorexia (anorexia has many psychological factors that are peripheral to the nature of this book and should not be seen as simply a problem associated with stress). Also we tend to burn far more calories in times of stress and worry because the brain goes into overdrive using as much as fifty per cent of your oxygen (approximately twenty per cent more than usual).

Vitamins B and C are badly depleted by the stress response so, during particularly stressful times it can be wise to take daily supplements of B and C to make up for the shortfall, and generally try to eat healthily.

## Increased Alcohol Intake

Alcohol is commonly used, and misused, to dull and suppress the effects of stress. When taken to extremes alcohol can be a stressor in itself because it acts as another adrenal stimulant. It also limits the flow of blood to the brain, in large quantities it shrinks the brain and combined with nicotine it can have a catastrophic long-term effect. It also triggers and exasperates the release of stress hormones (specifically hydrocortisone). Whilst you might find light temporary relief from a couple of beers, seeing it as the solution to your problems is setting yourself up for a fall. If you can keep your alcohol intake to minimum you'll probably be fine (it is hard to say because we are all different) but if you start to rely on alcohol to cope with stress then obvious problems are on the agenda.

## Increased Caffeine Consumption

This is one of the worst stressors of all. Caffeine acts as a catalyst and triggers the release of adrenalin in the same way as alcohol and sugar. Doctors believe that anything over five cups a day is detrimental in terms of stimulating stress hormones and affecting brain function. I know from my own experience, having suffered from long-term stress, too much strong coffee triggers my Adrenalin like nothing else, so now I only have decaff. If I feel very stressed I avoid coffee (or caffeine) like the plague.

## Constant Irritability

Irritability with others is a sure sign of stress; it is the body's way of trying to displace its stress. This is not good because it encourages contention and stress degeneration; it creates more stress than it releases.

One of the first signs that I am stressed is when I start feeling irritable with those around me or I feel easily offended or quick to anger, especially when I am in the car. These signs always let me know that it is time to pull back a little on my workload and find a Safe Surrogate Release. If I feel irritable with my wife (she always senses it anyway, and me with her) I always apologise and tell her why I feel irritable. Then, depending on how I'm feeling, I will go to my room and meditate, catch forty winks, go for a run or do something else physical to release my stress. Either way I always end up feeling better afterwards and my family doesn't get the brunt of it.

Recognising the signs is important, as is accepting responsibility and not allowing your unconscious defence mechanisms to displace the blame elsewhere.

## Suppressed Anger

As I said earlier suppressed anger can be very caustic to the internal smooth muscle tissue (heart, lungs and intestines) creating greater possibility of long-term illness. The anger, and Rogue Hormones, needs to be released in a controlled manner. People often tell me how they hold back their anger, how they lock it in, as though this was a good thing. It isn't!

Don't do that. If anything it is very bad. Holding it in is not so much an act of self-control as it is an act of madness. Holding all that sludge inside you is crazy. I agree that it does take a lot of self control not to take your stress out on others, and I admire that quality in people, but holding it all in is not good for you, it has to come out somewhere.

It is no different to putting a plug up your backside and holding all the waste in your body. At some point it's going to explode whether you like it or not. If not it may damage you internally. So find a safe release and let that baby go. Releasing Rogue Hormones and suppressed anger is, psychologically, like going to the bathroom to get rid of the toxic waste of the day. A crude example I admit, but the best example I can find.

## Increased (or First Time) Substance Misuse

People will always try and find a quick relief for the symptoms of stress because of its uncomfortable nature. One of these is the use of drugs. When people are stressed they are in pain and very vulnerable, this is when they are likely to grab for any relief they can find, even if, in the long-term, the source of that relief is detrimental to their well-being.

## Permanent State of Stress

This is possibly why drug abuse is endemic in our society. There are so many vague and intangible stressors constantly flying around us that we seem in a permanent state of stress.

And it is often easier to take a quick-fix suppressant than it is to make decisions to change our lives and make them less stressful.

Whilst temporarily numbing stress for now, in the long-term drug misuse creates an abundance of its own stress because of the health and social problems that drug taking incurs. The drug cocaine for instance imitates fright, triggering sympathetic nerves (the nerves associated with fight or flight) that can and has killed many users. It also leaves holes in the brain you could play marbles in. Other drugs, including the supposed safe drug marijuana act similarly. Any kind of serious suppressant, no matter how you rationalise it, is a downward spiral. Nobody has ever found the right solution with drink or drugs.

## Problems with Decision-making

To continue from what we have just said; it is often the ability to make strong decisions that enables us to release many of our stressors. One of our biggest problems as a species, unfortunately, is the inability to make these decisions. Sometimes the only way out of stressful situations (business, personal, confrontational) is positive decision-making. Without it our troubles often perpetuate; and the bigger they grow, the more open we are to further stress and the harder decision-making becomes. Also, stress has a habit of courting apathy, which leaves people not only unable to make decisions, but also not even wanting to.

Add to this the fact that the brain is using up twenty per cent more oxygen than usual and you can understand why decision-making becomes impaired and unstructured. Alcohol and drugs impair the brain and also take decision-making out of reach.

The brain is really no different from the body in that, if you overwork it, it becomes tired and its ability to operate at full capacity decreases.

The great problem with the contemporary stressor is the fact that it rarely needs a physical response. The brain, whilst not necessarily needed for running away or fighting, is needed for what becomes an analytical, strategic, decision-making battle fought in the mind every day of the week.

Whilst it is slightly peripheral to this book I would have to say that, over a long period, this can have catastrophic effects upon the sanity of highly stressed people. If we are constantly being exposed to symbolic stressors and our fuels, both mental and physical, are constantly being exhausted, the body and brain will start to find other sources of reserve fuel, just to survive. Whilst the body seems able to last quite a while without good nourishment, the brain does not and can atrophy very quickly. When all physical fuels are exhausted nervous energy is drawn as a reserve. Once we start tapping into this baby it is a slippery slope downwards.

Also, during fight or flight, blood is temporarily drawn from non-vital areas of the brain (those seen as not vital in fight or flight) and pumped to the muscles. In the short-term the brain seems to be able to cope well with this, but in the long-term (long-term stress) the lack of blood (and therefore oxygen) in the brain can only have a detrimental effect on brain cells.

I have experienced this on several occasions (without knowing it at the time) and on each occasion I quickly slipped into clinical depression. Once you have reached the point where you are borrowing energy you are badly impaired both physically and mentally. Physically the guard is down and you are vulnerable to numerous illnesses because the immune system is also impaired. Basically, you'll probably get whatever is going around. The immune system cannot protect you properly because it is weakened; it's on a skeleton staff whilst stress is on the agenda. Selye, whilst talking about the general adaptation syndrome (GAS) said he was particularly interested in the negative effects that prolonged stress exposure has on the body's resistance to disease and illness.

Solomon (1969) also showed that another outcome of the GAS seems to be a lowered resistance to illness, and a tendency to feelings of fatigue and general weakness. Long-term psychological effects, Solomon found, have also been identified, taking the forms of increased irritability and a tendency to have a pessimistic outlook. This is often referred to as burnout, which he found affects people in stressful occupations like the helping professions; social work, security, the city, teaching and nursing. The general adaptation syndrome is produced by the long-term stress that these people are under. This can have the effect of reducing their resilience and their experiences often mean they are powerless in their working situations, augmenting and exaggerating their stress.

If physical impairment is not bad enough, the fact that the body is not protected, and you subsequently pick up illnesses, becomes just another stressor straw on the proverbial camel's back.

## Losing the Plot (Psychosis)

Similarly, only more alarming, the brain is also badly undermanned by the stress response and the guard is either down or non-existent. Because the guard has gone (or been lowered) it becomes very difficult to function on a level playing field. Normally the healthy brain has the ability to filter out the rubbish that is floating around and stops it, at a conscious level, from filtering into the subconscious and becoming real. Normally if someone tells us something ridiculous (Martians are taking over the planet, for instance) we will probably say (or at least think), 'I'm not having that, it's a load of rubbish!' and we stop it from reaching our subconscious, therefore stopping it from becoming real. But when our brain is weak and impaired this filtering ability is often lost or badly weakened, subsequently whatever rubbish is floating around the cosmos we take in and it becomes our reality (the Martians really are taking over the world). The guard is down, the window is open and we are highly vulnerable to negative suggestion.

Liken your brain to a nightclub. You put four very strong bouncers on the front door to stop the bad people from entering the club. The club stays healthy and enjoys a happy existence. If the doormen are weakened, perhaps you knock them down to two people, the ability to stop the rubbish at the door halves. If you take away the door crew completely, all the rubbish can get in because there is no filter system.

I know of many people in the martial arts (just as an example) who have fallen foul of the weakened filter by over-training. They used up all their reserve fuel by grossly over-training until the guard was well and truly down – that's when the rubbish starts to get in. All of a sudden they become neurotic, psychotic, schizophrenic, paranoid or overtly nervous. Many of them hit such a low that they even started to hallucinate; and no amount of rational conversation could convince them that what they have seen, heard or felt is not real. What they imagine becomes their reality. This often becomes an obsession and, eventually, many of them commit suicide. They can see no way out and the downward spiral takes them to the very bottom of their sanity. Only the very strong, or the guided, get back up again.

When the mind is weak and the guard down it becomes difficult to filter the rubbish as it tries to enter the mind, this is possibly how cults and weird religious sects get their members, by feeding their philosophy into a temporarily unguarded mind. What they are told or what they are exposed to becomes their reality. They will argue for eternity that what they believe is real. And to them it is. But proof of reality is a very subjective matter, and in the context of this book it matters not. What does matter is that we have to stop the rubbish from getting in by keeping the guard high at all times. This means not allowing stress degeneration. You do this by not borrowing energy from the nervous system.

Keep the guard high at all times.

If you are on the other side of this and the rubbish has already entered you need to get it back out again. You do this by starving it. That is, paying no attention to it at all, and concentrating instead on positive and optimistic things. If you are in this position it is likely that you are grossly over doing it in some area (or perhaps all areas) of your life. This must change. Use the sixty per cent rule and never employ more than sixty per cent of your energy for work, and always keep ten per cent for reserve. In other words, stay balanced.

If your head is muddled and you're not sure whether what you are thinking is right or wrong ask yourself one thing. Are my thoughts positive or negative? If your information is dark (in that it makes you feel bad as opposed to good, sad as opposed to happy) don't try and analyse, prove or disprove it, just move away. It's like swimming around a fish bowl wasting energy. That's the trap. The more you overthink on that downward slide the more stress you create and the more compounded your problems become. So stop moving down and start moving back up again.

Some things in this life cannot be proved or disproved, even by the greatest scientific minds.

It has entered the unconscious raw and unfiltered and become actual; not good if the message is a dark one.

I won't pretend that this is my area of expertise because it isn't, so I won't go any deeper than I understand. All I will say is that I have experienced this phenomenon to the level we are talking about here and I have witnessed it many times with friends and peers. It is real and it is happening to people all over the world, so if it is happening, or has happened to you, welcome to the club, and take heart, you are definitely not on your own out there.

It can be avoided, and if you are there right now there is a way out.

## A Solution

This particular solution is simple in concept, but takes great exercise of will to make actual.

## Avoidance

Firstly we have to avoid. Don't allow the guard to drop; if the window is not open then negative energies can't enter because the sentry of your rational mind stops them. We avoid by keeping a good balance in our levels of energy. This means that if we work hard we must also play and rest hard. Don't overwork. Eat very healthily, avoid overthinking on a conscious level – thought drains the energy quicker than anything else, especially when you are going around the fish bowl trying to define something that cannot be defined. Try and keep large amounts of stress out of your life, if it comes in make the right decisions to get rid of it. Try to get plenty of fresh air and make sure your influences are high (as in positive). These include the people you associate with, the books that you read, the music you listen to, the programmes that you watch. Avoid low influences (as in negative). These should also include the people you associate with, the books that you read, the music you listen to, the programmes that you watch.

What we concentrate on becomes strong, what we ignore loses its power and dies. Concentrate only on good and pay no attention to bad.

## Humour

It's hard to see fun when one is stressed and yet, ironically, humour is one of the best stress busters around because it changes the perception of our stressors if we can laugh at them. Hearty laughter is also a molar action that can act as a Safe Surrogate Release. This is why black humour is developed in hardy jobs like the building industry, the mines, the door and the army. You have to learn to laugh in the face of danger if you are going to survive in environments like those. I can remember working as a hod carrier on the buildings. It was a murderous job, very stressful. Most new starters on the job never lasted longer than a week. One new guy didn't even last until the end of the first day. At about 1 p.m. one of the bricklayers was shouting for some more bricks but the new carrier was nowhere to be seen. Then one of the lads spotted him running across a field adjacent to the site. We were working about 50 miles from Coventry at the time so how the lad got home I'll never know. We never saw him again; he didn't even come back for his wages.

To survive the stress of this work we all developed (like the many generations of builders before us) a very black humour and would see fun in just about every subject. It's what got us through the day. Those that did not develop the crack (as we called it) did not survive in the trade. Similarly soldiers in wartime develop a black humour to help them through adversity. One incident I read about told of a chap who had his leg blown off by a landmine, the leg flew through the air and landed by his friend. 'I've lost my leg!' he screamed out to his mate. 'No you haven't,' his mate replied, 'it's over here!'

Laughter is a good escape from stress; if I'm ever feeling down and stressed I love to watch a funny film. Or I might ring or visit friends who make me laugh. When I was going to America last year to teach I got very stressed before the trip. To lighten myself up a little I went out and bought a collection of my favourite Laurel and Hardy films (I'm actually smiling now just at the thought of the hilarious duo). Watching them gave me a great laugh and really helped to take the pressure off me. Isn't it amazing that both Stan Laurel and Oliver Hardy are both dead now and yet they still give out so much energy via their films.

Books are the same, you can read (and I often do) books by authors that have been dead for hundreds of years and yet their energy is as alive today as it was then. Energy is immortal and always available, you just have to know how and when to get it.

## Concentration

It is hard to concentrate during stressful episodes (or before and after) because the brain lacks fuel. This makes concentration difficult. When we can't concentrate we get irritable and this becomes a source of frustration and anxiety, which creates more stress and uses more energy that we don't have.

What I tend to do when I can't concentrate is, I stop trying! I take the time out to relax, perhaps meditate or pray, maybe read a book, watch a film, whatever does it for me. This gives the brain much needed respite; once rested and refuelled it becomes much easier to concentrate. If life gets too stressful and I have loads to do I just beat a hasty retreat, grab a cup of something nice and have an hour to myself. When I return I feel rested and the task doesn't seem so impossible.

## Paranoia

This is a very real problem associated with stress (long-term stress specifically) because it makes us see problems and stressors that are not really there. This in itself creates more stress. Paranoia is due to the sentry on the conscious mind being weak and impaired, or non-existent, because we have used our primary source of energy and gone into borrowed energy. As your mind becomes rested and refuelled the guard or sentry can re-establish itself and irrational thoughts can be blocked at a conscious level, or weeded out at a subconscious level. It's important that you notice the signs of paranoia and stop it in its tracks. Again, if you let it get a grip on you it can be hard to wrestle yourself free.

As a highly stressed nightclub doorman I suffered many bouts of paranoia and found myself fronting situations (both mentally and physically) that were inventions of my own impaired imagination. This in turn created more stress for me because I would overreact and exasperate situations.

My friend who ran a public house had similar problems. If someone walked into his bar who perhaps looked a bit rough, or he hadn't seen them in the pub before, he would, in his stress-induced paranoia, allow his mind to see a threat that didn't really exist. He would anticipate trouble so much that it affected his behaviour toward the suspects. In the end it would become a self-fulfilling prophecy.

I have fought thousands of battles in my own head due to paranoia. In my minds' eye I have imagined fight strategies and game plans with potential attackers, what I would say and what I would do if my suspicions were right. Many years ago I nearly hit a guy in the gym. He kept looking over at me very aggressively (I thought) and I remember thinking 'this guy is going to have a go in a minute!' I went through every conceivable scenario of how he might approach me, what he might say or do if he did and what I would say or do to counter him. By the time he actually did approach me in the showers (a bit worrying I think you'll agree) I had already fought him a hundred times in my head. As he approached I thought, 'here we go. As soon as he goes for it I'm going to eclipse him.' He said, 'You're Geoff Thompson aren't you?'

'That's right!' I replied bluntly.

'I just wanted to say how much I loved your book *Watch My Back*, it was a very inspiring read.'

Well, I nearly dropped my soap let me tell you. I've never felt so embarrassed and so rude in all my life. The guy I was going to eclipse turned out to be a fan of my work and the only reason he was looking over at me was because he admired what I had written. I wanted a hole to appear so that I could disappear into it.

On another occasion Big Neil, a fellow doorman at the very stressful Busters nightclub in Coventry, got a paranoia attack. He had recently fallen out with his girlfriend and moved out of her flat, which only added to his stress, and was expecting her to visit the club to bring the remainder of his things. When her car drew up outside the club we all noticed a male companion in the passenger seat of the car. Normally this would not have bothered Neil, he was hardly the jealous type, but tonight, revved up with stress hormones and highly paranoid, the passenger was a red rag to a bull. Before we could stop him he raced over to the car, dragged the hapless victim out of the seat and punched him in the face. Neil's ex went mad and dragged him away. 'What are you doing', she screamed, 'hitting my cousin?'

'I thought he looked familiar' Neil admitted later.

## Feeling Unable to Cope

The feeling of being unable to cope is a very common one that can cause a fall in levels of self-esteem and lead to apathy. This becomes its own stressor because of the imagined sense that one is useless.

Being unable to cope usually occurs because the mind and the body have exhausted their fuel supply. Like a car without petrol it can't go anywhere. Sometimes we find ourselves with too many stressors, more work to do than we can actually cope with. In this case the inability to cope is actually real. In this kind of scenario it is important to make decisions quickly to lighten the load. I have been here many times in my life, you feel as though you can't lighten the load because in doing so you might let other people down. At one time in my life I was running weekend courses for self-defence, writing full-time, training twice a day, teaching weekday classes, writing articles, books, producing videos and trying to get a film made. As well as trying to maintain a family life. I had too many things to do and not enough energy or time to do them. I was getting exhausted and was in a constant state of stress. I felt that if I could stop teaching my weekend courses I could at least have Sundays off to rest. That would be enough. But I was stressed about not doing my courses because I felt I'd be letting people down. I was also worried because it meant less money coming into the house. But the bottom line was that I was unhappy and no amount of extra money was going to change that fact. I made the decision to stop the weekend courses for a while to lighten the load and, even though it was only one thing, it made a huge difference to my quality of life. I had more time at the weekends with the kids, I had at least one solid day where I could recuperate and reward myself for a hard week and I had taken away the stress of teaching hundreds of people. I rang the people up who had booked courses with me and apologised for cancelling them, explaining my time problem. To my surprise and delight they were all fine about it, they completely understood.

If you've got ten things on the agenda but can only manage eight, make the right decision and get rid of two. Do it right now before things get worse, the longer you leave things the harder it gets. And don't worry, it's not as if you can't pick those things back up again when time and energy permit.

## Feeling Out of Control

This feeling, again, is created by stress but also creates its own stress, because one of the greatest fears we experience as sentient beings is the fear of losing control.

As with many stress-related problems this one is brought on by a tired and unguarded mind that needs rest and nourishment. Nourishment, or energy, comes from three things: the food we eat, the air we breathe and our influences; keep all three fresh and high.

## Inability to Complete Things

Will-power is greatly depleted by stress and the inability to finish one job before going on to another is common. It is also another source of stress because it can cause contention in the work place or the home. It also promotes the feeling of being useless.

When I was stressed early in my first marriage I hated myself for constantly starting jobs that I couldn't finish. It hammered at my self-esteem because every time I felt inspired or got a great new idea I would subconsciously remind myself (or my superego would remind me) of all the other great ideas that lay unfinished in my past. This created a lot of stress for me. I became very frustrated and angry at my inability to reach completion. It also became a negative yardstick for my own ability to succeed in the future. I had left a trail of failures behind me, not because my ideas were not good, rather because I simply never finished anything. I was also reminded of this fact by friends, sometimes family, who would scoff at my latest ventures. 'What hare-brained scheme are you getting into this time?' This would take the wind right out of my sails.

I turned it around, but it took massive determination to start finishing everything that I set out to do so that in my wake lay a history of success and not failure. I got myself back on the upward spiral, so much so that in the end people would say, 'Geoff always finishes what he starts.' In fact, just recently one of my very close friends said to me, 'you'll be a millionaire Geoff, because you always achieve everything that you set out to achieve.'

If you have trouble with finishing big jobs, start on something small and build yourself up. Some jobs might take five minutes, others might take five years. Those that can be done quickly, get them done and dusted, those that might take five years get started as soon as possible, because that five years will disappear in a heart-beat, whether you are on the job or not. Were you ever on the verge of starting a long-term project and then suddenly thought, 'naw, I can't be bothered, its going to take ages!' The next thing you know 'ages' have gone and you're sat in the very same place, no farther forward in life, thinking, 'if only I'd just started when I said I was going to – I'd be there now!'

It happened to me years ago (and more than once before I learned). I always wanted to get my black belt in judo, but I knew that it would take two or three years of hard work and dedication, so I kept putting it off because three years seemed like forever. Then all of a sudden six years had passed me by and I found myself thinking, 'if I had only started judo when I first thought about it I'd have that black belt by now.'

Life goes by, whether you are using your time or just lounging around waiting for things to happen, so you may as well get busy and make your time as profitable as you can.

As a matter of fact I actually did get my black belt in judo in 1998.

Napoleon Bonaparte summoned one of his Generals for an urgent meeting. He ordered the General to make arrangements for trees to be planted down the sides of every major road in France. This, he said, would enable his soldiers to march for longer hours in the shade during the hot summer months, covering greater mileage than if they were forced to march under the sweltering sun. Perturbed by this request the General complained, 'But sir, it will take at least thirty years just for the tress to grow.' Bonaparte looked up from his desk and replied, 'Then we'd better get started right away, there is no time to lose.'

## **Lack of Hobbies**

One of the first things we lose during times of stress is the ability to have fun or pursue a hobby. It all starts to seem too much like hard work. This is because the will atrophies when the brain lacks energy. Ironically fun and the hobby horse are great stress busters; they occupy your mind and give it a little holiday from stressful thought – but not if you stop doing them. William Blake said that 'the busy bee had no time for sorrow.' Never was there a truer statement. In the worst case of depression I can remember experiencing as a youth, reading became my salvation and pulled me from the depths of despair. I read and read and read. Even when I didn't feel like reading I disciplined myself to grab a book and read. I didn't know why at the time, only that I always felt better afterwards. Even if you can't concentrate and don't seem to be taking the book in, do it anyway. It's like meditation, it focuses the mind on something other than the worries of the world. Don't read anything too heavy or demanding otherwise it'll become a chore and labour to an already tired brain. Keep it light and fun, something funny or fantastic, or escapist or inspirational.

Once you get into it I guarantee absolute bliss. I used to struggle like mad to concentrate on reading now it is my most treasured pastime. If you don't have the discipline, develop it by making yourself do a little every day until it becomes habit.

## Easily Tearful

Crying is one of the ways the body finds to release stress and, like all the other symptoms, one of the first signs that you are overdoing it. Because we associate crying with sadness, as opposed to therapy, we allow it to become a stressor, 'there must be something wrong with me, I keep crying.' This is especially so with men who might associate crying with weakness. I hated crying when I was younger and absolutely despised myself after I'd shed a tear. I remember feeling devastated and depressed after crying episodes. I felt I'd lost the plot, that I was a weakling, that I was (dare I say it) not a real man. Now I cry at the indigestion adverts.

Crying can be good, try to see it as a positive release, even sit down and watch a sad film to make yourself cry, you'll feel better for it. Crying works a lot of major muscles too (molar action), which can help to release Rogue Hormones.

## Constant Tiredness and Exhaustion

Sleep is the time when most major bodily repairs are undertaken, it is also rest time for the mind. If our sleep is not deep, or if it is broken we will, understandably, be tired the next day. For the body repairs to be made the body needs a good supply of nutrients as well as rest. Often these nutrients, although ingested, are not available because they have either been used as emergency fuel in the stress response, or they have been excreted straight through the body without proper ingestion. The latter might also be a side effect of stress (irritable bowel etc.). These vital nutrients might not even be in the body in the first place because stress often dulls the appetite, so we do not take in enough food. No supplies, no repairs. It's very logical really. Again, it's like a car, if you don't put fuel in the tank it won't go. If you don't make essential repairs the car will break down. We are not dissimilar. What you put in is what you get out, reap and sow and all that.

Lack of sleep is caused by the fact that a stressed body is in a constant state of arousal. The stressed person can be likened to a runner poised at the starting block in anticipation of the start gun that never seems to go off. It is sometimes impossible to sleep whilst the body is still so alert.

When I was depressed as a young man I found night-time to be the lowest and loneliest point of my day. I dreaded bedtime because deep sleep always seemed to elude me and worries surrounded me like hungry vultures. I'd always wake up very early in the morning, after a fitful and restless night, feeling worst than I did the night before. If I did sleep, it was in fits and starts and I'd suffer from bad nightmares and night terrors. Due to all of this I often found myself exhausted and tired in the day, to the extent that I would fall asleep at the most inappropriate times. Due to the lack of sleep my stress levels elevated and I found myself on the stress degeneration spiral. Even the fact that I couldn't sleep became a stressor to me because I constantly worried about it; and the more I worried the less I slept.

As I advised earlier, release the Rogue Hormones out of your system and sleep will come easier. If you are not sleeping well don't add to the problem by worrying about it, that'll only exasperate it. I know it's very easy for me to say 'don't worry', like you can just switch it on and off tap-like. I know it is not that simple. But what I realised and what I know is that worrying about sleep serves only to chase sleep away. I changed my perception on sleep; I started to think 'well, if I can't sleep I might as well do something productive while I'm lying here.' So I started reading in bed. I stopped trying to sleep and instead concentrated on getting through a book. I found that sleep came far more readily when I tried to stay awake than when I tried and go to sleep. Don't let the worry of sleep beat you up, stand up to it, tell it that you don't care whether or not you sleep, in fact tell it that you don't want to sleep, you have far too much to do. See how quickly sleep comes when you pretend that you don't want it. What we resist persists, so stop resisting and it'll stop persisting. It is not the lack of sleep that takes all our energy away (most people can live with a lot less sleep than they think), it's the inner conflict that our sleeplessness causes. We worry about not being able to sleep, and the stress it causes not only pushes sleep farther away from us, it also steals our energy and makes us more tired.

I read about a guy who was shot in the head, during the Second World War. The bullet never killed him but it did have a very strange effect, it took away his ability to fall asleep. The professionals at the time thought this disastrous, believing that the lack of sleep would kill him as sure as cyanide tea. Not so, he experienced no ill health due to his lack of sleep and lived to a ripe old age. All he did when his limbs were tired was lie, or sit down and rest. Many world leaders manage fantastically furious life-styles on very little sleep. Margaret Thatcher is said to sleep only four hours a night, and yet she still managed, amazingly, to become one of the most powerful and influential people in history.

Lack of sleep only really becomes a problem when we start to worry about it. No one in the history of man has ever died from lack of sleep, though many have popped their clogs through worrying about it. So if you can't sleep, don't allow it to dominate your thoughts because it is not the lack of sleep that makes you tired, rather it is worrying about the lack of sleep. If your body really needs to rest, believe me it will rest, whether you want it to or not. I remember when I was working late nights in the clubs having to survive sometimes on three to four hours sleep a night. When my body was tired it'd send me to sleep in a hurry, more then once I actually fell asleep, completely against my will, standing up by the DJ console.

So don't worry, the fact that you are not falling asleep means your body can do without it, otherwise you'd be asleep. Let the body tell you when it needs rest, and when it does tell you try to listen. If you can't sleep, stop trying, close your eyes and just rest, or meditate. The body actually gets more recuperation when you meditate than when you actually sleep. Don't worry, worry is the enemy.

## Low, Decreased or No Libido (Sex Drive)

Most of life's pleasures often become 'too much like hard work' when stress is on the agenda. Sex also can often take a back seat, especially if the recipient becomes apathetic. Libido probably drops due to the fact that sex is seen as a non-vital commodity during fight or flight and so the drive to procreate is temporarily switched off until the source of stress has gone. Often in a highly stressed life-style it never does (unless we learn to manage it). Stress has even been known to induce impotency, which to many men is a huge threat to esteem.

It is very hard to maintain arousal when your mind is awash with exterior (or interior) stressors.

Sex also demands a lot of physical and mental energy and focus; this is also difficult to achieve when the body and mind are exhausted. As with sleep, the more you think about lack of libido the bigger the problem becomes (or the smaller it becomes if you are a man, if you get my meaning).

Paradoxically, some people experience increased libido, especially men, and find themselves constantly wanting sex, or masturbating frequently. This is probably due to the fact that the hormones released in fight or flight are very similar to those released in sexual arousal. If the threat (in fight or flight) is not real and the hormones are not behaviourally released it is plausible that increased libido will result. Sex, I have found, is also a very good surrogate release for Rogue Stress Hormones (when you can get it), because it constitutes a molar action (even in masturbation) and thus utilises the Rogue Hormones. This could also explain why men in particular become aggressive if they are sexually aroused but the sex act does not take place (they are turned down for instance). [4]

Because sexual arousal is not dissimilar to stress arousal, post rebuttal aggression (in my opinion) could be seen as a manifestation of the 'direct aggression' release (if they take their aggression out on the source of their rebuttal), or displaced release if they take the aggression out on others. Men are notorious for being aggressive when they need sex, especially when they are not getting enough. And no end of problems occur if other unconscious defence mechanisms start clicking in.

Speaking from experience, I know how I have felt (especially as a younger man) when I was sexually aroused, but with no physical outlet for my urges. It made me very moody, irritable and aggressive, my appetite was dulled and although masturbation was a bit of relief it did not and could not take the place of full intercourse. This is why I find porn movies bad for health; the level of arousal is usually much higher than the release you get when you masturbate (or even have full sex) so you are left with loads of Rogue Hormones in the body. For those with little or no social conscience or no outlet for their arousal, the watching of these films, I believe, could lead directly to negative displacement, sex attacks and rape of innocent victims. I know this is a controversial thing to say but it is my opinion.

## Physical Symptoms and Conditions of Stress

This is a list of some other general physical symptoms and conditions that occur as a result of the stress response, especially with long-term stress. Bear in mind that these things can be avoided once you understand stress and start to avoid it or work it out of your system. They are listed in no particular order of importance and serve simply as a guide.

Migraine

Insomnia

Depression

Heart attacks and angina

Strokes

Peptic ulcers

Anorexia nervosa

Obesity

Eczema and psoriasis

Diabetes

Anxiety

Irritable bowel syndrome

Ulcerative colitis

Pruritus (bad itching)

Hay fever and allergies

Arthritis

Hyperthyroidism

Indigestion

Stomach cramps

Nausea

Flatulence

Heartburn

Constipation

Chest pain

Headaches

Palpitations

Jumpiness

The shakes

Fainting

Nail biting

Nervous twitches

Foot tapping

Premature ejaculation

Infertility

Menstrual irregularity

Failure to reach orgasm

Cold fingers and/or toes.

Increased baldness

Back pain

Neck pain

Cramps and spasms

Weight loss

Frequent urination

Enhanced feeling when wanting to urinate

Increased asthma

Tuberculosis

Other infections

Frequent colds and flu

If you are reading this list and cannot find your ailment, don't worry, this list is not comprehensive by any means. The stress syndrome can and does affect just about every part of your body from head to toe.

My mum was telling me about her recent visit to a stress counselling class. She told me how the instructor placed a huge sheet of paper on the floor, in the shape of the human body, and asked each member of the class to mark the paper with a pen at the point where their stress manifested.

After a few minutes every one in the rather large class (it was filled with young and old people from just about every walk of life) had made their mark on the paper body. My mum was amazed. There wasn't a single place on the body that someone had not marked.

What this tells us is that stress can affect you anywhere and everywhere and at any time. The greatest problem for many stressed people is the fact that, because their mentality and will is lowered by the stress response, they often think that every ache and pain they feel is a serious and life-threatening disease, usually cancer.

I have to confess that I have died many painful deaths in my mind, and from just about every ailment you can think of from testicular cancer to a brain tumour. And these phantom illnesses always seemed to strike when I was stressed.

I remember one time when I was overworking and overtraining and overthinking. My whole body was just one big ache, but of all the aches my testicles were the worst. I knew it was stress but my mind was so weak from overwork and under nourishment I started to convince myself that it was more serious, perhaps cancer. Then I made the mistake of reading an article in a woman's magazine called 'Detecting Testicular Cancer in your Man.' I read the symptoms and, within a day, I was testicular cancer man. I developed just about every symptom associated with the disease. I had it, I knew I did. I even got them out and showed my wife (oh the embarrassment!). I said, 'What do you reckon to these then?' She said, 'I beg your pardon?' I said, 'These! Do they look swollen to you, because they feel the size of coconuts to me?'

'Geoff,' she said, giving me one of those 'you've been reading women's magazines again' looks, 'you're stressed. There's nothing wrong with you. And if you don't believe me go and see the doctor and he'll tell you the same.'

Of course I didn't believe her, why should I, she wasn't a doctor. So I went to the doctor, just to put my mind at rest. I explained how I was feeling and that I thought it was stress, but would he examine me anyway, just to be sure? So I got them out again. 'What do ya reckon? Are these coconuts or what?' He didn't appreciate my wordy vernacular on the testicular but he did give me a once over and confirmed that 'no they're not coconuts and yes, it is psychosomatic.'

'Psychosomatic?' said I.

'In your mind!' said he.

'Well as long as it's not in my Y-fronts,' I thought.

The amazing thing was, as soon as he confirmed my health, the aches disappeared and I felt as right as ninepence.

This whole episode taught me never to let myself get that low again, not to allow the window to open if you like (and definitely not to read women's magazines).

Once the guard is down and the window open it is very difficult to stop the rot from creeping in. So the key is to be proactive and stop it before it starts.

It is very hard for the immune system to fight against the viral cells that attack our bodies when it is impaired due to constant stress, so stress reduction and avoidance (or management) has to be seen as a long-term commitment. It has to become a part of your life so that you can avoid being impaired and too weak to defend against the bad energies in the world.

# Chapter Nine
# The Defence Mechanisms

If there is one thing I have learned and one thing I know it is that stress has to be pulled out into the open and dealt with. It is a killer if left unattended so we must act, and act now.

If only it were that easy!

Over a lifetime of having to deal with stress, and largely because of its uncomfortable nature, the one thing most of us have not done is pulled stress out into the open, neither have we dealt with it very well. Rather, we have developed unconscious defence mechanisms to keep anxiety-producing impulses out of conscious awareness. The discomfort motivates the individual to avoid or reduce stress in any way they can, though not necessarily in ways beneficial for the long-term health and happiness of the individual.

At best, defence mechanisms are respite from stress. At worst, they are hidey-holes that keep the world out, but also keep us in.

Because anxiety is very uncomfortable it cannot (usually) be tolerated for long periods so we are highly motivated to do something to alleviate the discomfort.

## Direct Coping

One way of achieving this end is by addressing the cause of anxiety directly to avoid or stop the discomfort – this is called direct coping. Whenever possible this is definitely the best way to deal with the majority of stressors.

## Defensive Coping

We can also employ other non-direct methods called defensive coping, which includes various ways of distorting ones perception of the stressor to make it (appear) less threatening. 'If I ignore it it'll go away.' That sort of thing.

## Suppressant Coping

Or, as mentioned earlier, we can deaden the anxiety by means of suppressants such as drugs or alcohol.

Some people employ a combination of direct coping and defensive coping.

Defence mechanisms do not change the objectivity of an external stressor (they do not make the threat any less real), only the way that we actually see it. All defence mechanisms involve an element of self-deception.

## Denial – The Ostrich Complex

The most basic or primitive of these defence mechanisms is denial of reality. We block out the stressor by refusing to acknowledge it.

It's like the story of the ostrich and the lion. The lion is looking for a bit of lunch and happens upon the ostrich wandering around on its own. 'That'll do for me' thinks the lion and starts stalking the ostrich, setting up the kill. Just as the lion is about to pounce the ostrich spots the lion and shoves his own head deep into the sand. The lion, looking very puzzled, says 'where'd he go, where'd he go?'

Denial of reality is what I like to call the Ostrich Complex. When the ostrich feels threatened it buries its head into the sand believing that, if it cannot see the source of the threat, then the threat cannot see it, and is no longer real and therefore not a threat. Like the mother that denies the illness of her own child, despite expert and professional diagnosis. A less extreme example is the person who consistently ignores criticisms or fails to perceive that others are angry with them.

Paul was a very talented singer, though he was frightened to death of entering competitions and singing on stage to an audience. Rather than accept his fear on a conscious level and deal with it he used denial as a method of coping. He convinced himself and others that he was not scared of singing on stage, he just didn't want to do it (he said). Whilst this defence mechanism helped him to cope temporarily (his mind was not very strong at the time and could not accept on a conscious level that he was actually scared), in the long-term it stopped him from pursuing a career as a singer. It wasn't until years later that he finally accepted his fear and entered as many talent competitions as he could until the fear dissipated.

When you look around, you can see all of the defence mechanisms in every day use and sometimes they serve us well in that they increase satisfaction in daily living and are, or can be, helpful modes of adjustment. It's only when they become dominant modes of problem solving that they indicate personality maladjustment.

For example; if I'm watching my diet but I fancy a little treat (a cake or something) that is perhaps not on my diet sheet, I can rationalise my little treat by telling myself or others, 'I didn't have time to make anything healthy. A cake is better than eating nothing at all.' Or, as I always used to say to Sharon through mouthfuls of Madras and Miller Ice, 'One beer and a curry isn't going to kill me!' And as a one-off it probably won't do any lasting harm, but if I allow weak rationalisation to dominate my whole diet I might have a real health problem in a few years time when one beer becomes a six-pack and my six-pack becomes a beer barrel.

It can be very difficult to pull the problem out into the open when it is deeply imbedded into the subconscious and hidden by an abundance of defence mechanisms. Many, probably most, go through a lifetime without fully realising or accepting responsibility for their stress because the defence mechanisms – trying to protect the organism (you) from discomfort – hides or displaces the source deep in the annals of the unconscious mind.

Firstly it is imperative we understand our use of the defence mechanisms; secondly we must accept responsibility for dealing with stress on an external and positive level, and thirdly we must actively try to combat, or cope with, our stress. The more we can become conscious of ourselves the more we will grow in power and competence; after all, information is the base to everything.

Categorising, or listing the defence mechanisms, enables us to accept and understand how our own body and mind works. It gives us a better understanding of our own mechanics. Also, to name them is to take away their power.

## Rationalisation

Our source of stress might be the fact that we did not get the job we applied for, so we cope with our rebuttal by saying, 'I didn't want the job that much anyway!' when in fact we really wanted the job like nothing else on earth. The teenager who is stood up on a date says, 'I don't really care, she had big ears anyway.'

We rationalise firstly to ease our disappointment and secondly because it provides us with acceptable motives for our behaviour when a good excuse is needed.

If I wanted to buy a stolen television from some guy in the pub, but feel guilty because it's a little hot, I might rationalise my actions by saying, 'it's all right, everyone buys stolen goods.'

If we can convince ourselves that our crime is the norm it somehow makes it more acceptable, when really it's not.

When we rationalise to ease disappointment it doesn't really do us any harm, it helps us to cope in fact, but when we rationalise to justify a wrongdoing alarm bells start to ring.

## Nostalgia

Rather than face the problems of now or the future, many people choose to live in the past and hide in bouts of nostalgia. They also tend to view the past with rose-coloured spectacles and only remember the good old days. It's fine to visit the past now and then, nostalgia can be quite nice, but living in the past is no future for anyone. We must never forget that the past is dead and so we should, as Blake so eloquently put it, 'drive your cart and your plough over the bones of the dead.' In other words, leave the past behind you, face your problems in the present, using the past as a reference point if needed, then move on. There is no life living in the past.

## Specialisation

This can be good respite for those in a stressful environment. It is the art of temporarily distracting yourself from your stressors by taking a mental or physical break. This gives the brain time to recuperate. I do this by engrossing myself in a book, or with meditation, or by taking a few days away on holiday whenever I can. It has to be done for the sake of long-term health. If you are going to work hard then you need to rest and play hard too. But don't hide in specialisation, it is a place of respite, a holiday home, not a permanent abode.

## Compensation

This is the art of looking at what you've got and compensating it with what you haven't. We should all try to adopt this philosophy, it has tremendous benefits.

We are so very lucky in life to have so many wonderful things, and should thank God for what we have rather than procrastinate about the things that we don't have. We all have a lot more than we imagine.

I was on the verge of a big book deal many years ago and, to my disappointment, I didn't get it. For a while I felt very down about the knock-back until I realised that I had many good things in my life: the book deal could wait. The book deal would have been nice; the icing on the cake, but it wasn't everything. I was so very lucky; I had great health, a vocational job as a full-time writer, I could train whenever I wanted and I had a fabulous family. I started to look at all the things I had instead of looking at the things I lacked. I realised how very flattering it was to even be considered for publication by such a world-renowned publisher. Just to be in the running with such a global company meant that I was in prestigious company.

I also realised that I didn't make the sale because at that time it was not meant to be and when it is, it'll happen.

## Depersonalisation

Another coping mechanism is depersonalisation. If we do something we innately know is wrong, but can convince ourselves that no one is really affected personally by our misdeed, we can pretend that it is OK really because no one got hurt.

We can kid ourselves all day long that a misdeed is all right, but really we know it isn't. Using the same 'buying a stolen TV' analogy we might depersonalise the deed by saying, 'It's not as if it came from someone's house, it was stolen from a shop and everyone knows that shops are heavily insured. The shopkeeper will probably claim for twice as much on his insurance as was stolen.'

This suggests that whilst stealing from a house might be personal, stealing from a shop is not. My uncle ran a bicycle shop in a rough part of Coventry; his shop was robbed on numerous occasions. Please believe me when I tell you that every single time was very personal to my uncle and his family. Not only did it affect his business and his income it also badly affected his health because it made him a nervous wreck. As for the insurance, he was robbed so many times that his insurance rates went through the roof. Many companies would not even insure him because he had a bad history of being robbed.

By all means buy stolen property if that is your bag, but don't pretend that it isn't personal; it is, very.

I have also heard the very weak rationalisation of, 'I only steal from those that can afford it.' Oh really, that's so gracious! Again, this is as good as saying that because someone might be wealthy they are fair game, and it's their own fault for daring to be successful.

An up-and-coming young writer offered Debbie and John, two film producers, a great script. Rather than pay the guy for his work they turned him down and then developed his idea themselves. I felt that this was no better than breaking into his house and actually stealing it from him but they depersonalised the issue by saying that it was a cut-throat business and that 'everyone in film does it.'

## Inverted Depersonalisation

This is a defence mechanism that I use a lot and I find it very good for helping me to cope when life gets in my face. It's a lesson I learned from a friend in America called Benny Urquediz, a very famous martial artist, film actor and choreographer. His advice to me was 'don't take any of it personal.' And now I don't. If I am driving down the road and a guy cuts me up (or I inadvertently cut him up) and he starts shouting abuse at me or giving me the finger, I don't take it personal. I know that he doesn't even know me, he probably can't even see me properly through the windscreen. I also know that I am unlikely to be the source of his aggression, rather a displacement figure. So it isn't personal and I refuse to make it so because if I do it becomes my problem.

The only downside to inverted depersonalisation is the fact that sometimes it *is* personal and it does need to be addressed and defended. And in some cases people use inverted depersonalisation as a defence mechanism to avoid having to directly address a problem. For instance, there are a few people in Coventry who have taken a dislike to me because of my books about the violent door scene in the city. I don't take that personally, they don't even know me. Some of them even threaten me via the grapevine, but I don't take that personally either because I know that it's insecurity, ignorance or fear talking (maybe even the beer) and very unlikely to develop any further than pub talk. So I let all these kinds of thing go, and it honestly doesn't bother me. But one young man allowed his dislike for me to overflow into my family life. He threatened my daughter. Now I know that whether this threat was personal or not, it was dangerous and needed addressing before it did become physical, so I found out where he lived and gave him a talking to.

I read a great quote by a chap named Thich Nhat Hanh that exemplifies my point: *'We should not look at or listen to the one we feel is making us angry and causing us to suffer. In fact, the main root of our suffering is the seed of anger in us. The other person may have said or done something unskilful or unmindful. But his unskilful words or actions arise from his own suffering. He may just be seeking some relief, hoping to survive. The excessive suffering of one person will often overflow on to others. A person who is suffering needs our help, not our anger.'*

It takes wisdom to know when it is personal and when it is not; 99 per cent of the time it isn't, so let it go.

## **Projection**

My friend was training for the Midlands professional boxing title at middleweight. When he jumped on the scales the morning of the fight he was seven pounds over the middleweight limit and, because there was not enough time to get his weight down before the match, he couldn't fight for the title. Rather than accept responsibility for the problem he told everyone that it was his trainer's fault because his scales were out. Knowing my friend as I do I could see that this was a classic case of projection. He was legendary for his inability to control his pre-fight weight. Secretly he was also scared of having to fight for a title. It was quite a big jump up in class, not so much physically (he was more than able on that score) rather, his struggle was in his mind, he doubted his ability to hold the title, and the responsibilities that came with the belt. He was suffering from Maslow's Jonah complex, or the fear of success.

*'We are generally afraid to become that which we can glimpse in our most perfect moments, under the most perfect conditions; under conditions of greatest courage, we enjoy and even thrill to the God-like possibilities we see in ourselves at such peak moments, and yet, simultaneously, shiver with weakness, awe and fear before the same possibilities.'*

Rather than pull out of the match (this would have been too much for his ego to bear) he allowed his weight to go over the middleweight limit, to such an extent that he would not be able to fight for the title. This way he could exclude himself from the title fight without physically saying

'I don't want to fight.' On a conscious level he could not acknowledge and deal with his fear, he used the defence mechanism of projection and placed the blame on his trainer.

Projection is a form of rationalisation where we project personality traits (or sometimes just blame) on to others. We do this to protect ourselves from recognising what we dislike about ourselves. Stingy people often hide their tightness by talking about how stingy someone else is.

Pete and Sarah, a married couple I know, are both very intolerable of each other, and yet neither will accept their marital intolerance on a conscious level. Pete constantly complains to his friends about how intolerant Sarah is, and Sarah complains to her family about how hard it is to live with such an intolerable husband. Both project their personality trait on to each other rather than accept their own individual problem and deal with it.

I have a mate called Sue who is very jealous, even malicious (to the point of being blatantly rude), about my success. And yet, last time I spoke to her she said, 'you know what Geoff, I can't understand why some of your friends are so jealous of your success. I think it's great, I have no problem with it at all.'

She does not accept her own jealousy; rather she projects it on to others.

If you can't accept your problems on a conscious level you will never be free of them.

## Reaction Formation

Mark was always slagging off homosexuals and if you ever mentioned homosexuality he would recoil in mock horror and pretend to heave and be sick. If we were out having a drink or a meal and he spotted an overtly gay person (come to think of it, he always seemed to be the first to spot them) he would make lewd gestures and jokes and say how sick people like that were. Last time I saw him he had a boyfriend on his arm.

Reaction formation is a defence mechanism that conceals hidden motives from the self by giving strong expressions to its opposite. By censoring or attacking pornography for instance, the individual may actually be fascinated by such behaviour but at the same time ashamed of their own fascination. In a bid to prove their purity to themselves and others they attack (he protesteth too much me thinks) and often wage war or campaign against porn. This is not always the case of course, there are some very genuine campaigners doing good for the community. Similarly, not all people who dislike homosexuality are latent homosexuals; but the most vehement and aggressive campaigners are usually the ones to watch out for.

## Intellectualisation

Intellectualisation is our attempt to gain detachment from painful or uncomfortable emotions (certainly those which are a threat to the organism) by dealing with them in abstract and intellectual terms.

Sometimes a degree of intellectualisation is absolutely necessary for those in society who must deal with constant life and death situations. The doctor or nurse who deals with human suffering on a daily basis can ill afford to become too emotionally attached to their patients if they are to function effectively. In fact I would go as far as to say that they probably couldn't function properly at all if they allowed themselves to become emotionally involved with every patient they treat. If they did they would take on the stress (it is very infectious) of their patients and end up on the stress degeneration spiral (for a great story about medical intellectualisation watch *Patch Adams*, starring Robin Williams on video).

There is a fine line though between employing intellectualisation as a positive defence mechanism and becoming cold and robotic. I have found many doctors to be unapproachable and cold because they use too much intellectualisation. This is an objective view and not meant as a criticism of the medical fraternity who often perform a wonderful and thankless task. Their coldness may be a result of desensitisation after seeing so many patients; we become just another illness as opposed to a sick and sentient human being in need of careful and delicate handling. Over-intellectualisation, in the case of doctors for instance, actually disables you from effectively doing what you are trained to do.

Intellectualisation can be good respite from overwhelming conditions but should not be used as permanent armour.

## Undoing

Undoing often involves rituals or actions designed to prevent, atone or actually physically undo some unacceptable thought or impulse. This usually involves a repetitive and ritualistic action; avoiding stepping on cracks on the pavement or performing certain actions or tasks for a fixed number of times, for instance. It is often what we are taught from childhood. Another example is superstitious people who associate spilling salt on the dinner table with bad luck and throw a little of the salt over their shoulder to undo it. Or if they say something they feel is tempting fate ('I haven't had a cold in years'), they find something made of wood, touch it and say 'touch wood' to undo their belief that the statement is tempting fate.

## Obsessive-Compulsive Disorder (OCD)

This is all rather light-hearted and doesn't really do any harm unless you believe it too much, then it can become Obsessive-Compulsive Disorder where your whole life becomes one of undoing and where almost every action you make involves a ritual or repetitive movement.

Just the other day I observed a chap in a local café with this disorder. It must have taken him about ten minutes to drink one cup of tea, because before each drink he had to stir his tea a hundred times (I counted).

A very mild version of this is (usually when we are stressed) checking the locks on the door several times when we go out or when we go to bed, to make sure that we have locked them. Once is fine, twice isn't too bad just to make sure because we can all be forgetful at times, but once it gets beyond this we find ourselves not sleeping because we constantly worry that we haven't locked the doors properly (even though we have checked three times already).

When I was about ten or eleven I had a mild attack of OCD. Every night I would say my prayers, so many for my mum and so many for my dad. Which in itself is nice. But then I got to thinking that if I had said more for my mum than my dad, or more for my dad than my mum, in some way the prayers wouldn't work and I'd be a bad person. I also worried that I wasn't saying enough prayers. So I gradually increased the number of prayers that I was saying and became meticulous about saying exactly the same number for everyone. Of course in the end it became too much. I dreaded going to bed because I had hundreds of prayers to say in my night-time ritual before I would allow myself sleep. And if I didn't say any prayers at all I felt as though I would attract bad luck. Fortunately I grew out of this silly habit, but it just goes to show how easily undoing can start.

The mind is a very powerful organ, more powerful than any of us fully realise. We are creators; we have the ability to create – for good or for bad. If we concentrate enough and believe enough we can (and do) make things happen, this is the power of positive thought. Paradoxically we also have the power to make bad things happen if we dwell on them too much.

## Self-fulfilling Prophecy

If we dwell on the fact that neglecting a certain ritual will bring us bad luck then it probably will, but not because we failed to undo, rather because we believed it was because we failed to undo. It's what's known as a self-fulfilling prophecy. Someone with irritable bowel syndrome, for instance, who believes (or is told and subsequently believes) that a certain food or drink will exasperate their condition, will make it so with their belief. Similarly if you believe completely that you are immune to the flu virus that is going around you will be immune to it. Last Christmas everyone in my family had a very bad flu, except my wife Sharon who simply refused to have it. And even though she was in very close contact to the whole family, especially me, she didn't get it. She said, 'I refuse to have it, I'm too busy to be going down with flu.'

I had another friend who read about an outbreak of some very serious life-threatening disease that was going around (he was very stressed at the time) and then convinced himself that he had got the disease. He was so convinced that he actually developed the physical symptoms for the disease and eventually had to go to the doctor for a professional diagnosis. When the doctor told him that his symptoms were stress induced they went away as quickly as they came.

So think positive and make good things happen and if you read or are told something that triggers negative ideas, stop the thoughts dead by telling yourself, 'I'm not having any of this, I don't believe it, it's rubbish!'

## Repression

This is the art of unconsciously pushing things to the back of your mind, so far in fact that it often creates total forgetting. This happens quite often when one is involved in a bad car crash or exposed to a highly traumatic life event that the conscious mind cannot cope with. It occurs very often in war where scenes of death and mutilation are so traumatic that many soldiers repress the memories.

Repression can cause many problems later in life as the suppressed impulses try to find their way back to the surface, often in another form. I read of one man who suffered terrible abuse as a child. His mother prostituted him out to paedophiles. He later (as an adult) repressed these experiences but they rose to the surface as a terrible hatred of dominant women. This eventually turned to murder and he went on a killing spree – of dominant women.

If bad memories are brought to the conscious mind and are still too traumatic to be dealt with directly then the conscious mind pushes them back down again. The unconscious mind is a dumping ground for all the stressors in life that we cannot directly deal with; it's as cluttered as a scrapyard. If we can deal with the bad stuff that we push to our unconscious then our unconscious mind offers beautiful treasures that connect us to God.

## Suppression

Similarly, suppression is the act of pushing things into the unconscious mind consciously as opposed to unconsciously, by actually refusing to deal with stressful stimuli. Often repression is not total and impulses find indirect ways of making themselves known. Most of the other defence mechanisms serve repression, protecting the conscious mind from awareness of partially repressed impulses.

Many marriages break down because couples (or certainly one party) refuse to acknowledge marital or personal problems, or even accept that problems exist in the relationship. Rather than face the discomfort of bringing things out into the open they suppress them, until eventually the marriage fails and it is too late. Generally this is not the end of the problem, it has to be met at some point, and if it isn't the problem manifests (after the usual courting period) in the next relationship.

Simon takes his insecurity and mistrust of women into every new relationship because he cannot admit, and therefore address his problem directly. If you mention it to him he counters with denial, projection and aggression. He usually manages to suppress his problem in the early stages of each successive relationship but once the honeymoon period is over it always comes back to haunt him.

He believes that no woman can be trusted and that they will all, eventually, have affairs behind his back. His mother had many affairs when he was a child, and his first wife ran off with his best friend. The first woman he loved and trusted, his mother, formed his insecurity at grass roots level, and the second woman he loved, his wife, confirmed it (in his own mind).

He deals with his fears of infidelity by having lots of affairs himself. He is so convinced that all women are unfaithful he has affairs to hurt them before they get the chance to hurt him. He also treats the women in his life very badly to keep them at arms' length. And he never tells any of them that he loves them, he's very proud of this because, he says, 'they always hurt you once you let them in and I'm never going to let that happen again.'

Invariably his ill-founded belief becomes a self-fulfilling prophecy. When each successive girlfriend leaves him (usually always because he mistreats them), or finds solace in the arms of another man his belief is confirmed and consolidated. He is stuck in this cycle of degeneration and seems unable to escape, but that's because he will not even acknowledge his problem.

How can you solve a problem you don't even acknowledge you have? You can't, you just keep re-living the same old scenario for the rest of your life.

## Displacement

Freud felt that displacement was the best way of successfully and satisfactorily handling aggressive and sexual impulses. The basic drive could not be changed (that is, we cannot change our aggressive or sexual feelings) but the object towards which those feeling are directed could. For instance, if John upset me and made me feel very angry, he would be the source of my aggression, and that cannot be changed. But by channelling that energy in another direction my aggression could be spent on something other than John.

I remember when a particular fellow, many years ago now, wrote a very disparaging letter about me into a magazine's letter page. At the time it made me very angry but rather than vent my aggression directly towards my antagonist I channelled it into a book I was writing. Because I displaced the negative energy in a positive manner, and not at the letter writer (who was entitled to his view) I changed the object of my aggression and the book was one of my best pieces of writing.

They say that some of the greatest artists and writers of our time were aggressively or sexually repressed individuals and that's why their work was so powerful, they displaced their aggression into their work.

Some boxers starve themselves of sex before a major fight and then channel that sexually pent up energy into their opponents. One of my female friends, a wonderful writer, used to be a very angry and explosive individual and some of her very best work was written whilst she felt angry at the world.

When I wrote my autobiography, *Watch My Back*, I was a very angry and violent man and that is reflected in the writing, it's raw and in your face. I displaced my anger with the world, my ex-wife, my childhood bullies and my anger with all those who had abused me in the past into the book, and now, eight years on it has reached cult status and hit the *Sunday Times* bestsellers.

In this respect displacement is good because it's constructive as opposed to destructive and also very therapeutic.

All aggressive and sexual tensions share one common factor: they are forms of energy, and we can use that energy anyway we please if we understand the concepts. It's like the petrol we purchase from the garage; once we've bought the fuel we can drive anywhere we want with it. We might acquire £20 worth of petrol to drive up north, but if we change our minds we can use the same fuel to drive down to the south or the east or the west. Anywhere in fact, as long as we have enough fuel for the journey. Similarly, once we have the fuel we can use it in our car, in our motorbike, we can use it in the lawnmower, we can even use it when we are burning our rubbish if we want to.

The body is very similar; we get energy from lots of different sources but basically, wherever it comes from, it is just fuel, what we do with it is up to us. Some people choose to waste their fuel with procrastination or by getting angry and aggressive over the small stuff.

Others become frightened of the fuel and its potential so they try to hold it in and end up making themselves ill. I choose to collect and refine fuel from many different springs and then redirect (or displace) it, into positive life goals.

My method of 'collect and displace' only becomes a problem when you are collecting fuel but have nowhere to displace it. I try to direct my energy into current projects, at the moment it's this book, or my life's goal at this moment in time, my screenplay.

So if your environment is giving you bundles of aggressive energy do something positive with it, write a passionate article, put it in oils and create a masterpiece, channel it into a work of sculpture or use it charitably to help others. Just because the energy comes in an angry package doesn't mean that it has to go out angry. It's just energy, contain it, refine it and drive it into your life. It was Harold Emerson Fosdick that said, 'No steam or gas ever drives anything until it is confined. No Niagara is ever turned into light or power until it is tunnelled. No life ever grows great until it is focused, dedicated, disciplined.'

The energy that life gives us in so many wonderful ways needs to be focused, dedicated and disciplined. But how can we do that if we do not even understand that what our influences offer up every single day of the week is energy? Unrefined, undisciplined and unfocused I'll grant you but energy all the same. This is the secret of perpetual motion; what we need to energise us surrounds us, and it is completely free, we just don't know it, and if we do we just don't use it.

Sir Bob Geldof witnessed the starving millions in Africa. He was so incensed, so angry and so very touched by the deprivation he made it his vocation to do something about it. He achieved what many would have deemed impossible; he raised millions of pounds by campaigning and raising public awareness to the plight of these unfortunate people. Mr Geldof is probably responsible for saving the lives of thousands, perhaps even millions of people. He refined and displaced the very raw energy he felt in the way of anger into a passion that literally moved mountains. As anger, that energy was of little use so he refined it and directed it into his campaign to raise money to help the dying.

My very overweight friend caught sight of herself in the reflection of a shop window and was mortified at what she saw. She couldn't believe how overweight she had become. She refined energy that came in the form of disgust and drove it into a campaign to lose weight, which she did. And if she ever felt lacking in energy she reminded herself of how she had looked that day in the shop window and her determination and resolve returned.

Look at the Bruce Lee phenomenon. Thirty years ago a nine stone Asian martial artist exploded on to our cinema screens and millions of people all around the world were energised into following a martial path. Thirty years on, and despite his premature death, Mr Lee still sells good copy. Why? Because he offers energy – in the form of inspiration – to anyone who wants to be a great martial artist (or indeed a great person).

## Sublimation

In psychological terms this might be called Sublimation, which can be thought of as a coping mechanism and a defence mechanism, because it involves channelling anxiety, anger, fear, whatever you want to call it (energy is probably the term I would be inclined to use) in socially desirable ways. This makes it both positive and constructive.

If you do not utilise the fuel with controlled displacement then it will invariably find its own way out in an uncontrolled manner, directly or indirectly. Or, just as bad, it might stay in the body and act as a toxic bath for our internal organs.

## Isolation

If life, or the people and problems in life, are your stressors then what better way to escape them than by isolation, by taking yourself out of life. But is that living? Probably not. Isolation, in part, might not be all bad. One of the best ways of lowering your stress levels is to avoid too much stressful stimuli; this is not only sensible it is also recommended. But to isolate yourself completely is to compound your problems because you become afraid of life itself. Before you know it you'll be afraid to leave your own house.

It is generally felt that all defence mechanisms can act as temporary defensive armour until we can mature and develop better problem solving abilities. It is only when these better problem solving abilities are not developed and the defence mechanisms become our only way of coping that they start to cause problems in our growth.

# Chapter Ten
# Coping Mechanisms

Running parallel with the defence mechanisms are coping mechanisms; these are the positive and conscious alternatives to some of our unconscious defences, they allow us to cope with stress in a more productive way.

Here are some positive alternatives to the major defence mechanisms.

## Logical Analysis Instead of Rationalisation

Rather than fall for weak rationalisation try logical analysis, and carefully, systematically analyse your problems in the search for better explanations and answers. Once explanations are found you can set plans to solve the problem based on the findings and the realities of the situation. John used to take all his stress out on his wife and when this started to have a detrimental effect on his marriage he sat down and analysed his problems. Analysis showed him that his workload was unbearable and that when he came home of a night all he wanted was to be left alone. This didn't help his marriage. If he wasn't left alone he found himself snappy and aggressive. He worked with this knowledge and changed not only his workload but also his perception to work (that he could enjoy it, or change it if he wanted to). He delegated more at work, and did fewer hours and always made time to talk with his wife when he felt tense or stressed.

## Self-Honesty and Concentration Instead of Denial

Denial was one of my favourite ways of not having to face the things I feared most as a younger person. I would frequently say, 'I'm not afraid of it, I just don't want to do it!' Instead it is better to be honest with yourself and admit (even if it is only to yourself) that you are experiencing natural apprehension (no shame in this, it is often mistaken for fear) and then concentrate on finding a way past the stressful stumbling block. This is the ability to set aside disturbing thoughts and then to concentrate on the task in hand, whatever that may be. There is always a way around things, it just takes a little effort.

## Empathy Instead of Projection

It is very easy to project our traits on to others, rather than accept our own shortcomings. Of course while we are projecting we cannot be healing, because we are not accepting responsibility. So empathy, as opposed to projection, is the art of sensing how others are feeling in emotionally arousing conditions so that we can interact with a full account of their feelings, and not project our traits on to them.

When someone gets aggressive with me I try to look at how and why they are reacting this way, as opposed to reacting similarly, then deal with them accordingly. I also try to examine my own feelings, if I feel I am using projection as a defence mechanism I try to nip it in the bud and deal with it. If we can imagine for just one second the pain that others must be feeling in times of stress we will find compassion in our hearts even for our enemies, and empathy would be easily employable.

## Playfulness Instead of Regression

Laugh and the whole world laughs with you, cry and you cry alone, as the saying goes. Making light of our stressors does make them seem less controlling and more manageable. Most of what we get stressed about, in the whole scope of things, are not really threats to the organism at all. It is only our perception that deems them so. It is our negative thoughts that allow wild imaginings to cultivate. Don't entertain wild imaginings, stay in the now and kill negative thoughts as soon as they try to enter your mind. Playfulness in times of stress is the ability to use past feelings or ideas and behaviour to improve the quality of our problem solving solutions, and also add a little fun to our lives. If we can learn to laugh in the face of adversity, and replace anger with laughter we are on the right track to a lighter and more fun existence. It is only when we start letting life get to us that it actually starts to drag us down.

Try to see the fun in everything, and everything will, you'll find, take on a look of fun.

When Sharon and I are the victims of road rage we refuse to get upset, we just look at each other and start to laugh, because we have learned to see the funny side of traffic aggression. Some poor chap that has had a bad day at the office wants to come to fisticuffs over a parking space or a bit of tarmac on the road. The really funny bit is the fact that we know more about him than he does about himself. And the fact that we know that he is trying to displace his aggression on us automatically disqualifies him from ever doing so. Where does the aggression go if we refuse to take it? Straight back to him of course because he is so angry at our indifference, at the fact that we are totally ignoring his aggression. We refuse to be pulled in. I also find it hilarious that these people are trying to get into an argument with us, and our jobs for the last ten years have been teaching self-protection. I have trained every day of my life to deal with people of this ilk. If you think about it, they couldn't really pick a worse pair to have a fight with.

Don't forget what I said earlier about collecting and refining energy; if you do allow others to rouse your anger and you use it to argue or fight you'll be wasting energy that is far better used in other ways. Energy is currency; don't throw money down the drain by investing it into an argument over a space in the road.

Once you start to understand the rules of play, and understand what is going on out there, it gives you a head start on everyone else because you are party to information that the greater majority is not. This nurtures an ability to function well in stressful situations where others might struggle. The more pieces to the jigsaw you have (the pieces are the information that you accrue) the more the picture changes and the clearer it becomes.

So look for the humour in everything and things will become lighter. Everyday you must practise on the events that challenge you. Humour (often black humour) has taken many men through life and death environments. Laugh, laugh, laugh. It's all a game anyway, so play the game right back and don't get caught out.

## **Suppression Instead of Repression**

We have established that regression is a long-term problem, one we'd rather not have. A temporary alternative might be suppression, the ability to consciously (as opposed to unconsciously) forget about, or temporarily hold back thoughts and feelings until a more appropriate time and place presents itself to express them. This might entail pushing the thoughts about one matter to the back of your mind whilst you deal with a current situation. Later, perhaps at a more appropriate time you can then deal with the original problem.

These are just a few alternatives, there are many more that you can find, even make up, for yourself and as long as it works and it does no harm then do it. Nothing is cast in stone, life is malleable, you can change it, tailor it, mould it so that it fits your idea of nirvana. By recognising the defence mechanisms that we unconsciously use we are better able to understand our own weaknesses. This enables us to search for information, which helps us to deal with things on a conscious and positive level. In the long-term this will enable us to live a happier existence.

If we deal directly with our problems as they arise we won't be carrying them around like dead bodies. Situations arise all the time in life, and they all offer information and energy, they all hold learning potential, but only if we face them. If we do not, and instead employ defence mechanisms as a long-term solution, we are going to carry their burden internally, and be forced to face the same problems again and again until the lesson is learned, or we exit this world unfulfilled.

## Chapter Eleven
# The Buck Stops Here: The Safe Surrogate Release (SSR)

If stress is a physical syndrome then, logically, it needs a physical (or behavioural) release. If this is not forthcoming, for whatever reason, we start to experience tangible problems, either by way of the toxic bath caused by Rogue Stress Hormones or negative displacement. The buck has to stop somewhere if we are ever to escape from this stress.

I believe the answer, certainly on a physical level, is the Safe Surrogate Release. This is a way of releasing the Rogue Hormones (trapped adrenalin) in a positive and safe way. This is achieved by means of a molar action – a physical activity – something that mimics flight or fight and acts as a surrogate (or substitute) release.

In theory any activity that is molar (bodily actions that involve several muscle groups like running or dancing), as opposed to molecular (small bodily actions like picking up a cup, or walking to the car) will act as a good surrogate release, but in fact not even molar action acts as a de-stressor.

For the safe release to be effective it has to be a non-contentious activity, something that we enjoy that is not stressful, otherwise we end up back on the stress degeneration cycle. For instance, if I tried to take my mum running to release her Rogue Hormones it wouldn't work, because my mother, as an older person (she's two years older than water) and a definite non-runner, might find running a tremendously stressful experience. This being the case she would incur more stress than she releases because the exercise itself becomes a stressor. So it is very important to find an activity that serves the dual purpose of offering enjoyment and release. My in-laws do this by going swimming and dancing (both at the same time which is a bit of a worry!). Both swimming and dancing are molar actions and neither are stressful activities (to them).

This is a very personal thing of course, what might be stressful to one may be enjoyable to another and vice versa. It is therefore very important to find an activity you enjoy.

Some of my friends on the door play squash, others golf, both molar activities that are non-contentious (unless you make them so by becoming too competitive). One of the activities I found myself participating in through a particularly stressful period of my life was ice-skating. I found it very enjoyable and a great release for my stress. My friend Ian, also a doorman, came with me for the same reason but he allowed it to become competitive, he started playing ice hockey. He encouraged me to do the same but I refused because there is not a single part of ice hockey that I find relaxing. Now I don't know if you have ever watched an ice hockey game but, basically, it is less like a game and more of a mass brawl with big sticks – they just bash the shit out of each other for a couple of hours, it is a scrap on ice. I don't know about you but that to me is hardly a relaxing, molar action to release stress hormones. To me it was more like a life or death battle with a hockey stick.

Ian went into hockey whilst I stuck with recreational skating. As I expected he got into loads of ice-fights and become more stressed than before he started. I didn't and enjoyed my skating as a means of de-sludging the psychological and physiological shit from my system.

Some activities (like ice-skating was for me) can also be very good because they are meditative in that they encourage focus. Basically when you focus hard on one point (fishing is a good example but for the fact that you have to kill small animals with very sharp hooks!) it gives your conscious mind a rest, a holiday, a vacation. It is respite for the mind. Sometimes that's all it needs. My favourite way of focusing my mind is reading. I love it, love it. As a young and heavily depressed man, reading was my absolute salvation. It got me through some very difficult times. I have a friend (don't worry John Smith of Bell Green, Coventry, I'll keep you anonymous) who was very depressed for about a month, a long time to be down let me tell you. My one piece of advice to him was to take up reading. He rang me later saying how much better he felt, though he wasn't sure why. I asked him what he was doing that was different. 'Nothing,' he replied, 'only reading, I've been doing a lot of reading.' I rest my case.

Negative thought is our enemy; it is a very energy consuming pastime. Even if the thoughts are not negative they can be very energy consuming. Concentrating hard for long periods on some enigma can absolutely empty the tank. This is especially so when we are stressed already and our energy levels are low. Constant and repetitive thought, for example going over and over a situation that has occurred or may be about to occur, uses masses of energy that we haven't really got so we start dipping into and borrowing from reserve energy. As I said earlier, it's a bit like spending all the money you have in the bank, using your overdraft and then, when that's all gone, still trying to draw on an empty account. The account collapses. Similarly, when we no longer have any energy to draw on we collapse with depression or a nervous breakdown. These are not the traits of weak-minded people, rather they are the traits of energy deficient people.

Now in terms of psychology I don't know how well any of these concepts stand up, and to be honest I don't really care too much either because I know from experience, from having lived a whole lifetime with these problems that this is how it is.

So if you can avoid being overdrawn you can avoid the lower echelons of depression and the problems in life associated with this state. If you do have to go into overdraft, recognise that you are there and don't stay too long.

As we have said throughout the book, releasing the Rogue Hormones is very important if we are to improve long-term health and happiness. But we mustn't forget to also address the root cause of the stress because, if we don't, the stress will keep re-occurring. If our stressor is symbolic, problems at work for instance (as opposed to a physical 'mugger down the entry' type of problem), then this needs to be addressed.

The possible health problems associated with stress will eventually affect your quality of life.

The possible consequences of stress are obvious. Yet I know a lot of very intelligent people who are blind to the truth. If you suggest that they might be overdoing it and point out the risks some actually smile as though accepting a compliment and not a warning.

We shouldn't have to see death to appreciate life. The doctor shouldn't have to slap a diagnosis of dying on our lap before we finally get it.

I used to be proud of the fact that I abused my body with massive training sessions that left me crawling from the gym, proud that I was battered and scarred from my real workouts, delighted when people said 'you're overdoing it.' It is the quality of what you do that matters and not the quantity, and if you manage your time correctly you'll get a lot more done in the long-term.

Here are just a few lines on the physical effects Rogue Stress Hormones can have on the internal health of the body. This is information to help convince you to change your world and make it less stressful. Also, if you have been suffering long-term stress don't worry, your body has a wonderful habit of healing itself if you change your ways. It's not too late, so start now.

As far as the heart rate and blood pressure is concerned, chronic stress (that is, stress over a long period of time with no behavioural release) can evoke repeated episodes of increased heart rate and blood pressure, which in turn produces plaque formation within the cardiovascular system (shit gets left in the arteries and can clog the pipes). Stress also produces an increase in blood cholesterol levels. This is because adrenalin (and noradrenalin) triggers the release of fatty acids, which produce a clumping together of cholesterol particles, which cause clotting in the blood, in the artery walls and obstruction of the arteries. Due to the pipes being blocked blood cannot run freely through the arteries and this triggers a logjam so the heart rate climbs, which again is related to a more rapid build up of cholesterol on the artery walls. The subsequent high blood pressure results in small lesions on the artery walls that the cholesterol gets trapped in (Holmes 1994).

Basically this means that the residue of stress hormones which are not released from the body clog up in the arteries (these are the tubes that carry blood from the heart). When the heart tries to pump blood through these blocked or restricted arteries it creates a logjam and heart attack occurs.

It's like getting rubbish stuck in the sink waste pipe in your kitchen, the waste water cannot escape into the drain, so the sink overflows and floods the kitchen.

## The Immune System

Long-term stress has a detrimental effect on the immune system, which is one of the ways that stress may result in disease.

The immune system is a collection of millions of cells that travel through the bloodstream and move in and out of tissues and organs, defending the body against invasion by foreign agents (things like bacteria, viruses and cancerous cells). Stress reduces the immune system's ability to fight off such attacks, and often leaves the body badly defended against these potentially harmful agents. This is why people often become ill with colds and flu after heavy studying and exams, or if they work too hard or train too often. All these everyday stressors have a detrimental effect (certainly over a long period) on the effective working of the immune system. Studies have also shown decreases in the levels of lymphocytes (these are white blood cells, called 'natural killer cells', in the immune system that fight off viruses and cancer cells) among people experiencing intensive stress.

Bad health, via stress, is a real problem and today should be the day you start to make changes in your life so that you do not become another victim to the stress assassin.

## Chapter Twelve
# The Id, the Ego and the Superego

Much of our daily stress is brought on and perpetuated by ourselves. We often create our own stress with negative thought patterns, or our unconscious self perpetuates stress by hanging on to old stressors (or grudges) that may not have been directly resolved.

For instance, by allowing our negative thoughts free rein we often overanticipate situations and this creates anticipatory release of stress hormones into the body. Often, simply by looking at the stressor more realistically we can see that, in fact, there is really no need to worry at all. A pessimist might look at a forthcoming social event as highly stressful because he feels that everything that can go wrong probably will. And if his prediction is right (he feels) he won't be able to cope, he'll be embarrassed, ashamed, people might laugh at him, his self-esteem might even be attacked. And all because he overanticipates the possible negative consequences of his planned event.

The optimist would probably get no stress in anticipation of a social event because he believes everything will go according to plan and if it doesn't, 'hey, I'll handle it, it's not the end of the world.'

In truth (even if they do happen) most of the dire consequences we envisage, future imaginings that we allow to stress us out, will not change the course of our lives. It is only our perception that turns benign events into disasters waiting to happen. With practice, diligence and a bit of information we can alter our perceptions for the better, we can bring them to heel like an obedient pet. Then our perceptions will serve us well; they will change our world into a better place to live.

## Forgiveness

As for self-generating or self-perpetuating stress, this is one of the greatest enemies to the organism. Not only are we constantly experiencing stressors in the now, we are also re-experiencing stressors from the past (and often anticipating possible stressors for the future). Dwelling on past stressors is partly due to our inability to forgive others or ourselves. But this is going into the spiritual realms, and have you ever noticed that, when you mention things of a spiritual nature, eyes start to roll and conversational exits are surreptitiously sought? Is it, do you think, because the pietistic nature of the unseen does not align with our peer-pressured effigy of the bronzed Adonis? I've always had a deep interest in spirituality myself, though I admit through my woolly mammoth period it was buried beneath a tangible fear of looking like a twat in front of my mates should I ever be outed. Thus if spirituality came into the conversation I followed the norm and patronisingly eye-rolled with the rest of the sheep. Now that I am a little more self-assured I don't need the kind of conditional security that the norm offers, rather I look to developing a deep-rooted internal security that is as steadfast as it is empowering. And where I once toiled for surface mastery – hitting hard, moving heavy weights, looking good, building muscle – I now labour from the inside out, pumping cerebral iron to build a sinewy mentality. One of the hardest lessons I learned en route, which made me lighter and stronger for the practice, was the capacity to forgive. They say that forgiveness is good for the soul, it is the doctrinal mainstay of just about every religious icon, from the Nazarene right through to Mahatma Ghandi. And yet when we examine the world in which we live, and when we closely examine our own lives we see that there are many people preaching forgiveness, but very few actually putting it into practice. We claim to love those close to us yet we can't forgive our brother for a ten year old error in judgement, or our sister for some wrong she inflicted upon us last year. We can't forgive the foreman for the way he treats us on the factory floor, or our neighbour for a minor misdemeanour. And we definitely can't exonerate our ex-spouse for their ill treatment of us in a former marriage. It appears that we can't even forgive ourselves for solecisms made on our own journey through life.

Oh, sometimes we feign forgiveness with the anaemic proclamation, 'I'll forgive you, but I'll never forget!' or the equally unconvincing 'I'll never completely forgive you!'

But you can no sooner 'partially' forgive than you can partially fall out of a tree, you either do or you do not.

We also have a great tendency to rationalise our blame with inane remarks like, 'Yeah, but you don't know what she did to me, I can't forgive her,' and we seem perversely proud of ourselves, as though this were some great virtue.

It is not virtuous; there is no great feat of strength in carrying the carcass of a long dead argument. Holding a grudge is easy, you can do it without even trying. To forgive! Now then, that's a horse of a completely different colour. It takes strength, discipline and great understanding. I believe it is a great weakness in the human spirit that disables us from the active practice of forgiveness.

But what has this got to do with stress I hear you cry! Let me tell you. Our lack of forgiveness is killing us – literally.

Our failure to pardon manifests an umbrage that grows with the passing of time, it is an internal time bomb of bitterness triggered and perpetuated by every mind's eye replay. This has a catastrophic effect upon our physiology. Every time the grudge is replayed like an old movie it activates physiological fight or flight, that is, the release of many stress hormones into the bloodstream. Your contentious thought is registered by the mid-brain as a physical threat, a sabre-toothed tiger if you like. But – and here's where the problems start – because it is not a physical threat, just a reminiscence, behavioural 'fight or flight' is not activated – that is, we do not run or fight for our lives. So all those redundant stress hormones lie dormant in your body, like a toxic bath, wreaking havoc – even brain cells are killed by the Rogues.

Add to this the fact that your immune system is greatly impaired by the stress response, and therefore cannot adequately defend the body against infiltrating viral and cancerous cells, and you have a recipe for disaster, even death. It is already estimated that 95 per cent of all contemporary illness finds its roots in stress.

So every time your mind's eye relives past upsets your body actually re-lives them too – as though it were for the very first time. This means that someone who insulted you ten years ago, who you haven't forgiven, is still insulting you today and you're letting them!

Logically the best way to stop people from hurting you is to forgive them. This is what Charles Handy would call 'proper selfishness.' The exercise is not so much a means of helping the object of your grudge (though this too is laudable) rather it is to help yourself.

Once you forgive a person you stop carrying them.

In my younger days working as a nightclub bouncer, I held many grudges, and for several years. Every time I thought about my past tormentors I could literally feel the stress hormones racing around my veins, not realising that I was on a downward spiral to ill health. I am ashamed to admit that I was very proud of my aggregation of grudges and perennially laid them out on the table like favoured collectibles. I often bragged to others that 'I will never forgive,' and 'one day I might even seek revenge.'

When I finally realised what I was doing to myself, or more specifically, what I was letting others do to me, I instantly let go of the past and forgave those I had been carrying for so long. I felt as light as the proverbial feather, I also felt empowered. Now I always make a point of forgiving people when they upset my apple cart, I even try to forgive people proactively, before they do anything to upset me.

Start with yourself

Many people feel that forgiveness is a weakness, and this discourages them from any active practice. From my experience forgiveness is the shield and sword of the gods, is a great strength that should be nurtured in all people.

Like most things in life it is better to start small. Forgiveness needs to be localised, forgive the wee things and gradually build up to the big ones. Start with yourself. We all have cupboarded skeletons that perennially plague us; whatever they are, forgive yourself and move on.

As far as health is concerned this internal cleansing is an integral piece of the longevity jigsaw and if you want to stay fit for life, forgive the past and get on with living in, and loving, the now.

## Attack the Roots

Many people attack the leaves when they should be attacking the roots.

If I was in a boat with a leak I could use a cup to bail the water flowing in, and as a temporary measure this might work. But untended leaks have a habit of getting bigger the longer they are left. Soon the proverbial cup isn't big enough to bail you out; a bucket is called for. As the hole gets bigger still, even the bucket won't suffice. Eventually you'll be spending more time bailing than rowing. At this point the word 'Titanic' springs to mind – you are aboard a sinking ship. We need to attend to the leaks.

Similarly, we can find a Safe Surrogate Release for our stress and keep releasing it from the system (bailing the water) but if at some point we do not address the root cause (the hole) we are destined only to sink.

If my stressor is a friend's insult which has not been dealt with, I can displace the Rogue Hormones all day long and that'll bring temporary respite but it will not deal with the root cause; the original insult. So every time I think about that insult I get stressed and angry. At some point I'll have to deal with the root cause if I want to stop the stress. There is no point in suppressing or repressing it, or employing defence mechanisms, rather I'll have to deal with it directly. This way the conflict is put to bed permanently.

The insult can be dealt with in one of several ways. I could deal with it directly by approaching my friend and saying 'I am not happy about what you said, please don't say it again if you value our friendship'. I could try to understand why he insulted me, and forgive him; after all he may have just been having a bad day. I could put the situation down to experience and let it go. If the situation was serious enough to demand it I could also forgive them, but cross them off my Christmas card list, disinherit them as it were.

I had a friend who blatantly and maliciously insulted me. It really upset me. I looked at his insult every which way, and no matter how I viewed it the insult left me cold, so I stopped seeing him. If we bumped into each other I would be polite and respectful and then move on. I never held a grudge; I completely forgave him, I just chose to spend my quality time in better company from then on.

## The Id, the Ego and the Superego

Freud felt that stress or discord is caused by the conflict between the id impulses (the id is a part of the unconscious that is only concerned with survival and instant gratification), the ego (which is a kind of referee or mediator) and the superego (the internal parent, the voice that tells you when you are right and when you are wrong).

The ego, Freud claimed, develops purely to mediate between what id impulse demands (instant gratification at any cost) and what reality actually has to offer. Later, when the superego develops, the ego also has to take into account its demands, and barters between the superego, the id and reality.

The superego is like an internal parent and, it is believed, develops from around the age of five when it is formed by our immediate influences; parents, brothers and sisters, relatives, environment, culture and society. It tries to demand perfection in all things (perfection according to its beliefs). Even though it is instinctive to feel the urge to run from conflict (determined by the id impulse for survival) the superego normally still views running away as cowardly, and therefore unacceptable. This varies quite a lot from one person to the next, according to their beliefs.

The superego, like our biological parents, tends to reward us with high self-esteem and feelings of great self-worth when we act according to its beliefs and punishes us with feelings of guilt, remorse and low self-esteem when we act against them.

As a species this four-way skirmish (id, ego, super-ego, and reality) is probably our greatest source of inner conflict and energy loss. An almost constant battle inside our own minds. In most of these battles the id impulse usually wins the day because natural instinct is the strongest emotion we feel.

Natural instinct is generally much stronger in what it considers life and death situations, than the collective forces of both the ego and the superego. Relatively speaking, the ego and superego are just youngsters compared to the granddad id impulse that has been passed down from gene to gene for many generations.

To help gain a better understanding of this conflict it is not a bad idea to go straight to Freud himself to see what he felt on the matter (forgive me here if I repeat anything that I may have already said – I think it needs repeating).

He saw the adult personality as having three basic components: the id, the ego and the superego. The id and the superego, both unconscious, exert pressure on the ego, which is the part of the brain in direct contact with reality. Freud's theory was that as young infants we only have the id; the ego and the superego are developed later. The id is what we bring into the world when we are born; it is the primeval, impulsive part of the personality that demands instant gratification. It is the spoilt kid in each of us that is unrealistic, selfish and demanding. It works on the pleasure principal: every impulse should be satisfied immediately.

As we mature of course, reality kicks in. It informs us that, actually, we can't have everything we want immediately. We realise that some things are simply not possible, and it is necessary to make adjustments in order to achieve any of its desires. This is where the ego, a natural offshoot of the id, develops. It acts as a go-between for the id impulse and reality. It makes compromises with reality to pacify the id. The ego operates according to the reality principle and tries to balance the demands of the unconscious mind (id and superego) with what is practical.

As we mature we come into contact with authority and a world filled with rules, regulations, principles, duties, morality and honour. Our parents and other close influences generally impose these stipulations upon us when we are still very young. As we grow these rules become solid and intertwined into the personality. They become a part of who we are. So we actually develop what is termed as an internal parent who holds strict ideas of propriety, duty, conscience and obligation. This internal parent is known as the superego.

Whilst the ideals of the superego may be grand they are, in reality, often as unrealistic as the impulses of the id. Where the id is impulsive and overreactive, the superego is overdemanding in that it expects total commitment to the most rigid demands and regimes, even at the cost of its own well-being.

So the ego is the mediator, its role is to maintain a balance between the conflicting pressures brought to bare by the opposing or conflicting parts of the unconscious and also to keep on an even keel with the demands of reality. It maintains what Freud called a state of dynamic equilibrium between the opposing pressures in a constant balancing act. He also felt that the unconscious parts of the mind were constantly and continually trying to break through and dominate the consciousness, but are held back by the ego, which is in a constant state of threat from three sources; the id, the superego and reality.

In order to cope with these formidable opponents it uses the defence mechanisms mentioned earlier in the book. These are generally only used as a temporary measure until a better, more tangible solution can be sought. Unfortunately, and often, these are either not sought or not found and the defence mechanism become the unconscious norm allowing conflicts to bury themselves deep into the psyche, only to cause more problems later on in life when they reemerge in the form of illness or displacement.

## Ending the Conflict

Ending this continual conflict has been my life's aim; I work on it every day. To take away the conflict will demand great understanding and courage. It will also entail re-educating the mind so that it does not follow society's dictates, rather it listens to its own intuition, what it feels is right and wrong. This entails looking deeply at what our superego demands and questioning it so that the untrue dissipates. As it is we are led, pet-like, by societal demands that are more fashionable than they are practical, they are more concerned with exterior security than an internal locust of control. What is right and wrong should not be dictated by societal fad, rather it should be a holistically spiritual constant guided by our own intuition.

Most of our disharmony is centred on either survival (id – 'where's the next meal coming from?') or acceptance (superego – 'what do people think of me?'). Once we let go of public opinion and leave survival to whoever it is that looks over us we no longer need the ego or superego. With these gone conflict is redundant.

Just to reiterate; positive displacement needs to be backed up by a direct method of actually removing the cause of conflict, the original stressor. If you don't remove the source of the stress then you are only treating the symptom and not the cause.

# Chapter Thirteen
# Relief From Stress

My intention throughout this book has been to offer information, panacea and solutions to the problems of stress. Throughout the text there are practical ideas on how to avoid, escape and dispel stress. This final chapter offers a few other thoughts, which might also help to this end. Some of it is a reminder. I always find that when something is stated several times it sticks better.

Fear can come in many formats, from the shiver of delight that you get in anticipation of a forthcoming event to drenching, overwhelming terror, which is often inadequately called anxiety or dread. It can also manifest suddenly in life-saving fight or flight. Other times it can gnaw away at us endlessly and with little apparent cause, we think of this as anxiety. Other times, when we feel naked, alone and embarrassed we call it shame and are punished for our sins by the superego, with feelings of guilt. All of these emotions, whilst perhaps not immediately recognisable as fear, release the same chemical cocktail into the bloodstream.

What we perceive as fearful, and therefore stressful, is really not. It is only that we allow our thoughts free rein that the perception develops into a fully-grown, anxiety-producing fear. So the key is to control your thoughts and nip wrongful perception in the bud. We do this with the power of positive thought; something most of us find very difficult to do. It is easier, it would seem, to think negative thoughts than positive. The former race into our mind, uninvited and often unsolicited.

## Internal Dialogue

Our thoughts (internal dialogue) really do matter, they actually determine who we are and how we feel. Thoughts have a physical effect on every other cell in our body. Negative thoughts can have such an effect that, in extreme cases, they can kill us. In mild cases they can make us unhappy and miserable, even dominate our existence. They can affect our relationships, our work, our social life, in fact our whole lives. If you can train your mind to think only good thoughts then your whole reality changes for the better and you create a wonderful and fulfilling life. If left unchecked negative thoughts can crush you like a bug.

We can train our minds not just by courting positive thoughts but also by intercepting and stopping negative ones as soon as they are noticed, instead of allowing them access and entertaining them. You can catch negative thoughts at the moment they occur and correct them by disagreeing with them. Or question what they say and prove them wrong with positive affirmations – after all, not all thoughts are true just because we have them, in fact most negative thoughts are usually untrue, exaggerations or mere imaginings.

Thoughts are real, every thought we have sends an electrical signal through our brain, and they have actual physical properties that significantly affect every cell in your body. Every time you have bad thoughts (sad, angry, unkind, judgmental, cranky) your brain is affected in what is known as the deep limbic system and chemicals are released that make your body feel low and melancholy. Notice how awful you feel the next time you allow bad thoughts into your mind. Your muscles tense, your heart beats faster, your hands might start to sweat. Generally you feel terrible. When you think good thoughts however the opposite is true. Good thoughts, happy thoughts, kind and hopeful thoughts make your body feel good. Chemicals that bring happiness and the feeling of wellbeing are released into the system. Muscles relax, heart beat slows, hands become dry and breath steadier and easier. Your body reacts according to your thoughts, that's why it is essential to start courting good thoughts and stopping bad thoughts.

Many psychiatrists are convinced that stress (and stressors) is propagated by (and partly due to) faulty internal dialogues. Individuals fail to self-instruct successfully. Firstly you should become aware of the maladaptive nature of self-statements (how thinking bad thoughts can and do actually make you feel bad). Then you should set about changing the nature of these thoughts and self-speech with coping self-statements: when the negative thoughts enter your mind, notice them, question them. If our thoughts tell us that we cannot cope with a situation we should tell ourselves the opposite; 'I can cope, I can handle this, this is not a problem.' Change your thinking habits, and habits that might attract negative thoughts.

When facing a potentially stressful situation you can self-instruct pre-confrontation, telling yourself that you can deal with it, and that this situation is not a problem. If the feelings of anxiety start to come on stronger then challenge them. Feelings of anxiety and fear are self-perpetuating; initially the stressor causes us to feel fear, then we panic because we feel fear. So the fear of the feeling becomes the stressor. This then releases more stress hormones. In the end you actually become frightened of the feelings of fear as opposed to the object of fear and your mind is overrun by negative thoughts.

I used to be terrified of fighting in karate competitions but I couldn't work out why. I wasn't frightened of being hurt, I wasn't frightened of success, failure or embarrassment. In fact there was nothing tangible about karate tournaments that frightened me. What I mistook for fear was simply natural anticipation, but the feelings of anticipation caused me to feel fear, which triggered the release of adrenalin, which frightened me more. Before I knew it I was awash with stress hormones and unable to cope. Subsequently I bottled it and didn't enter the tournaments. I had allowed my inner voice to panic with the initial feelings of natural anticipation. I gave the thoughts refuge in my mind and allowed them to multiply by not stopping them right at the start. Eventually I had neither control of the inner voice (it tends to get stronger the more you let it control) nor the release of stress hormones. This, I am afraid to say, was the story of my young life and it didn't stop until I got a grip of the internal dialogue, once I did that I turned my life around.

Changing the way you think will change your whole life. It won't come overnight. If you have been allowing negative thoughts to run your head for the best part of your life you can hardly expect to change that habit in one easy lesson. It will take daily practice. But that's the exciting thing. Once you know how it works and how to stop it, it becomes a game. Negative thoughts become tennis balls flying over a net, you pick up your imaginary racket and smash them right back. Think of negative thoughts as flies around the jam jar that you swat away. Or what Daniel G Amen MD calls ANTS (Automatic Negative Thoughts). He says that you should notice ANTS as soon as they start to climb on to your sandwiches and crush them before they get a chance to ruin the picnic. He said that we should think of ANTS as pollution, every time you allow an ANT into your mind it is like you are drinking poison. Negative thoughts are mouldy bread, sour milk, and maggot-filled meat. Would you consider taking them into your system? Probably not. Negative thoughts are as bad, probably worse. So don't allow a single thought to go unchecked. Keep your mind clean or germs will grow. I practice this every day, it is very hard for a negative thought to come into my mind without smiling broadly to myself and then smashing them back with my imaginary tennis racket. I smile because I recognise them and what they are trying to do. The whole thing has become a game to me. I refuse to be taken hostage by negative thoughts; I stop them immediately before they have a chance to grow strong. I question thoughts as soon as they come into my head, use positive affirmations to shine light on the shadow of ANTS. When they come into your mind, smile and tell them, 'I know what you are and I'm not having any of it!'

Once I 'got it' I used to challenge the feelings of anxiety when they attacked by saying 'is that it, is that your best shot, the best you can do? I can handle this all day long, in fact give me more, this is too easy.'

This positive and challenging dialogue always stopped the stress degeneration in its tracks, and every time the feelings came I repeated the challenge, never allowing myself to succumb to panic. Panic is the cause of stress perpetuation. Don't allow yourself to start feeling like a victim, don't tell yourself that you don't like it, or that you want it to stop.

This panic is what worsens the situation. Panic and negative self-speech triggers the release of stress hormones. So trick it, tell it that you don't care, that you can handle it, that you actually like the feeling and 'thank you, can you send some more please?'

After the situation has passed give yourself a positive pat on the back and some good self-briefings of what you did right and how you might improve the next time. Every day practice positive self-talk, tell yourself what a great day it is, what a great life it is, even if it is pouring it down with rain tell yourself, 'this is great, it's beautiful, I love the rain. Snow? I can't get enough of it!' Never give up, no matter how bad you feel don't allow the negative self-speak to dominate.

## Thought Stopping

If you feel that the negative self-speak and subsequent adrenal release has gone too far and you are struggling to override them, you can try the extremely effective thought stopping. Wolp (1978) felt that whilst positive internal dialogue is effective (even imperative) in the early stages of stress, it was not so useful once severe anxiety had set in because many strong neurotic fears are triggered by objects and situations which the individual knows are harmless – this is why phobias are so irrational. He used a technique called thought stopping (this was mainly used with obsessive-compulsive individuals). The individual is told to actually dwell on his or her obsessive thoughts and, while this is happening, get someone (a close family member, someone that you trust, or in the absence of a second party, yourself) to shout 'Stop!' The individual then repeats the command out loud and eventually repeats it sub-vocally (in thought only). Then, every time that you feel the irrational thoughts or feelings shout out loud or in your head, 'Stop!'

Many people believe themselves to be victims, 'I can't do anything about it, and the thoughts just come and go at will!' They believe there is nothing they can do to stop the thoughts and feelings. Of course none of us are victims: to accept that we are is to place ourselves into a victim state. As we said earlier, this is learned helplessness.

The key elements in depression are negative thoughts about oneself, the world and the future. These thoughts seem to come automatically and involuntarily. The source of these thoughts is logical errors based on having been fed (or having self-fed) faulty data. Once negative thinking has been identified, it can be replaced by collecting evidence against it. For instance if I was depressed or stressed because of a forthcoming event, which I felt I couldn't cope with, I would find evidence to the contrary and use positive self-speak to convince myself that I could cope with it.

A couple of years ago I got very stressed about the fact that I had been invited to a very big public speaking event by a highly reputable organisation on the world stage. I started to panic thinking that maybe I wasn't ready for such a big event (it was an invite to the biggest event of my life thus far), maybe my standard was not high enough, maybe I'd be a flop. Even as an experienced self-motivator I temporarily allowed my self-speech to become negative and it was upsetting me, to the extent that I actually contemplated turning the offer down. To turn this around I quickly got a grip of myself-speak (actually I grabbed it violently around the throat and shook it) and started to accrue evidence to disprove its suggestions. I had done a thousand seminars that would be no different to this one. They'd all been very successful, I was the best in my particular field, I knew my stuff, I believed this categorically, and no matter whether the seminar was a success or a failure I would be there and I would handle it either way. Not only was I going to do this seminar but I was going to make it the very best I had ever done. I would make sure that my preparation was meticulous and I would leave nothing to chance. This was going to be a great trip. Every time ANTS came into my mind I noticed them and talked right over them with positive internal dialogue. I told myself how I had God in my corner and that no force in the universe was stronger than God's will. I dwelled on the positive aspects so much that I was starting to actually get excited about the event; I was looking forward to it.

And it was my best ever to date. I made it so. It was my most successful and it took me on to the world stage. We are what we think. So think bold, think grand, think positive and when the ANTS try to get in your pants think 'get lost!'

We have so much power as individuals, we can have anything that we want, we are creators (co-creators with God), we have the ability to create, and all we have to do is think it and believe it. And if you find it difficult right now don't worry; Rome wasn't built in a day (I think it took at least a week). Start practising what you think, start banishing negative thoughts from your mind, from the moment you rise in the morning until the moment you go to bed at night think, speak and act positively, you just have to re-train yourself, and the more you practice the quicker it will happen.

If you look at someone and think a negative thought (we all do from time to time) change it immediately for a positive thought. If you can't think of anything positive about certain people then say nothing at all. If you are building up to an event and negative thoughts start creeping in, laugh at them, shine light on them and watch them disappear. They are nothing unless you give them life by giving them attention. Let them know that they have been caught, then kick them out and change them for positive thoughts. Or just get your positive head on and talk right over them like they are not even there. And keep doing it until they go. The more you defeat positive thoughts the less power you give them. Courting them and listening to them is feeding them, making them grow fat until they occupy your whole consciousness. It's just a game really, and if you look at it in this light it will take the sting out of the tail.

Don't forget also that negative (or ignorant) people can also feed us their ANTS if we let them. How many times have you come away from a conversation with a negative person and felt really fed up. Or they have said something negative or dark that sticks in your head, making you feel bad for days. They are feeding you their ANTS. It has been medically proven that keeping bad company physically affects your brain and releases chemicals that make you feel low. This isn't the fault of the people who perhaps behave unskilfully; it's our fault for letting them. So choose better company, exit the company if the talk becomes negative or put up your bullshit guard if you are stuck with negative people. When they say stuff that might make you feel negative just say (or think to yourself if saying it might offend), 'actually that's a lot of nonsense, I'm not having any of it!' We don't have to sit and listen to rubbish. What we watch on the TV and read in the papers isn't necessarily true just because it says so. Yet we watch it all and rarely question the information. If we allow ourselves to be spoon-fed rubbish it's no wonder we feel like rubbish all the time. We can choose, so I say let's choose better.

If someone came up to you in the pub and said, 'Here (nudge nudge, wink wink), take this pill, only £20, it'll make you feel down for days,' you'd say, 'On your bike you weak specimen!' You would, I'm sure of it.

Also train to distance yourself from things a little so that you can be more objective, so that you can distinguish fact and fiction and fact from evaluation, so that you can see things in proportion. Often it is hard for the eyes to see clearly what the mind has got completely out of focus. Make all of your influences positive, model yourself on the positive behaviour of great people. I read a lot. I watch only positive and informative programmes on the TV. I listen to stimulating music. If art is your thing, surround yourself with paintings and sculptures of great beauty.

Don't engage in self-criticism (or criticism of others), admit your faults of course, but treat yourself how you would treat your most favourite person – no less that that – when offering constructive advice.

Also don't be afraid to admit that you have strengths. Many people are all too quick to tell you where their weaknesses lie, but will not tell you that they are strong in other areas. This false humility is not good. We need to accept our strengths in order that our weaker areas might model them. Always look for the positive in yourself, others and in everything around you. Everything has something positive, you just have to look for it. If you are too busy looking for faults you'll only see what you want to see. Be positive in all that you do and people will flock to be a part of your world. Like attracts like. I have read hundreds of books on business, on how to succeed, on the psychology of success, how to win friends and influence people and all the rest of it. And there have been some great books, I have learned lots. But I can give you the secret of success in one line. Get people to like you. It's that simple. People want to do business with people that they like and admire. You could have the best product in the world and still not do great business because people do not like you. People might disagree with me but I know I'm right. And the only way to get people to like you is by being entirely genuine. Not being a great person with a hidden agenda, not getting to know people because they have a great network, or they are a name or a face or a good contact. Get to know them and to help them because it is the right thing to do, irrespective of what is in it for you. Give with no thought of return. Give because it is good to give. Help others to get what they want and you will always get what you want.

## Be Assertive

Don't be afraid to be assertive in life. Say no sometimes. Many of us are frightened to say no because we do not want to offend people. But we only have a finite amount of time and that means that we cannot possibly help everyone. Just help those that you can. Sometimes you just have to grab the bull by the horns and say, 'actually no! I just haven't got the time, I'm sorry.' And when you say it, mean it. Not 'maybe', 'I don't know', 'I'll see what I can do', 'let me think about it', because basically that means 'yes, I can be talked into it.' Say no, mean no.

If it makes it a bit easier and you are worried about offending people, give them the reasons why you have to say no, but don't make up excuses and don't tell white lies, just give the plain facts and perhaps offer them alternatives as to who *can* help them.

## Write it Down

If you find you have lots of jobs running around in your head, write them down.

One of my big stressors used to be the fact that I always seemed to have a load of jobs to do and was constantly worried in case I forgot to do any of them. So I wrote them down in order of importance, this way I didn't have to keep juggling them around in my head. Then I set about ticking them off one at a time. Once written down I also realised that some of the jobs I thought important were not and could be either left permanently, left until later in the week or delegated to someone else. You also gain great satisfaction when ticking off each completed job; it gives you a feeling of achievement.

You find yourself looking forward to ticking off the jobs as each one is completed, whereas before you dreaded them. This concept turns a stressor into a challenge.

Many people see problems in everyday life as stressors, and therefore consciously or unconsciously avoid confronting them. But when we avoid the pain that problems bring we also avoid the growth that fronting those problems generates. I believe it was Benjamin Franklin who said, 'Those things that hurt instruct.' Every problem we encounter is not really a problem; rather it is an assignment sent from God to develop the soul. A problem in life is a bar-bell for building the mentality. So we should never procrastinate when rocks fall in our way, we must welcome the rocks because overcoming those rocks *is* the apprenticeship.

## Problems are Opportunities

We should always try to look at problems as opportunities, they help us to grow and they are not hurdles, they are climbing frames set to build our mentality and make us wiser and more erudite people.

You are always that bit stronger and that bit wiser when you overcome one of life's stumbling blocks. Life is an exciting series of challenges that should be looked upon with vigour and the bigger the challenge the bigger the spoils when it has been met and overcome.

## Work to Live, Don't Live to Work

Change your perception to work, you should be working to live not living to work. Don't let your job become so pivotal that your life falls apart if that job is threatened.

Often, when people lose their jobs or are made redundant (or perhaps they do not have a job in the first place) they feel useless and unneeded. It doesn't have to be like that, seek new challenges, set new goals, travel, learn new skills, get fresh training, go to evening classes, do a sport, anything to use time and bring direction and zest back into your life. The world really is your oyster; it is a very exciting place.

One of my friends went from having a nervous breakdown to getting a university degree. She only went back to school to keep busy, the next thing I heard she'd got the education bug and is now training for a masters degree. She has been without depression for over ten years now.

We all have the ability to change, to become the people we always aspired to be but we have to start with that first step, only *you* can make the difference; if you put your mind behind something nothing will be out of your reach, nothing at all.

## Replace Anger with Laughter

One of the most important things I've learned to do over the years is to replace anger with laughter. Things that once made me madder than a March Hare now make me smile, giggle or even laugh. Have a good laugh about life. It won't mind (honest).

It takes practice and tenacity. It is said that through repetition the magic will rise. If you want to change, you can and you will. Now is the time to start. William James advised us that 'to change one's life start immediately; do it flamboyantly; no exceptions.'

## Don't Race Against Time

One of my greatest problems and a terrible source of stress for me was the fact that I was always rushing around everywhere, always racing against the clock. And I have to say it made my life a misery. If I was due to meet someone at one o'clock I would leave about ten minutes early, and then find myself rushing like crazy to arrive on time, which invariably I did not manage to do. Now I always leave early for meetings and enjoy the drive, taking my time. If I have to travel far I don't even bother with the car anymore I go by train, it's just as cheap and takes away all the stress of driving and traffic. On the train I'll get a cup of tea and a biscuit, read a book or a magazine or just look at the beautiful British countryside out of the carriage window. I actually love travelling by train; it's great (and who cares if they are late, more time for tea and cake).

## Realism is a Must

If you are setting goals of course it is nice to aim for the top, but be realistic with what you have and where you want to be. You can get anywhere, be anywhere, do anything, but sometimes it takes planning and pyramidic steps. When

I first started my publishing business I wanted the best of everything, from paper quality to full colour covers on the books, top design, advertising and experienced reps to get my books out there. I had loads of ideas for books and wanted to get them all out at once. These were great aims, but totally unrealistic on my finances, I just did not have the financial muscle to do the things I wanted right off. So I started by getting the best I could with the money I had. I released one book, which was all I could afford at the time, and the publishing company I was working through (Summersdale Publishers) kindly kept their typesetting and distributing prices low enough for me to manage. All the money I earned from my first book (except for a few pounds that I spent on sweets and pop) I ploughed back into the business to finance the next venture. Later, when I could afford it, I also republished some of my first books to a higher standard. Eventually I had over 50 products to sell, and all of a high quality.

So being realistic doesn't mean aiming low, it means aiming to the top of what you can afford at the time, and then aiming higher the next time and the next time.

## Circles of Influence

Don't worry about the things in life you have no influence over. Some things are inside the circle of our influence, which means we are in a position to influence and change them if needs be. If they are inside and they're a source of stress do the very best you can to change them for the better. If they are outside the circle of your influence this means that, no matter what you do, they cannot be changed; you have no influence over them whatsoever (an aeroplane falling out of the sky on to your house when you are having your tea, for instance). If this is the case don't worry about them; don't become stressed over them because it is energy thrown down the drain that could be used on something positive.

When workers were digging the road up outside my house it was potentially very stressful, many of the neighbours got really uptight about it because of the constant noise and the mess that the workers left every day. But the bottom line was, they had to dig the road up, there were problems with the gas pipes and no matter how much we complained they were still going to dig and mend the pipes. It was outside the circle of our influence. Why worry about something that cannot be changed? Accept it, ignore it, live with it. If however, the neighbour's children keep running over your newly planted daffs and this is a stressor to you then, because it is inside the circle of your influence, have a quiet word with their parents, and ask them to stop (please).

If it is inside deal with it, if it is outside accept and live with it.

## Listen and Learn

Try to listen to others without rushing them, finishing their sentences, or nodding as though to say 'yeah, I get the picture!' One of the most therapeutic things you can do for yourself is to help others, and a big part of helping others is to listen and only offer advice if it is asked for. Let them talk as much as they want without interruption, and try to keep the conversation based around them as opposed to you. There is nothing worse than talking about yourself and about how well you're doing and what great deals you've got coming up when the other person perhaps feels as though their life is going nowhere. Try to highlight people's strong points and base conversations around them. If you think they need inspiration do your best to inspire. If they need a spiritual lift (and you have it in you) tailor your conversation accordingly.

Be a listener rather than a talker, you'll be surprised at how much you learn when you listen.

## Relax and Have a Laugh

Learn to relax more, laugh every day, and even make yourself sit and watch a favourite film that makes you giggle. Take time out to practice meditation or yoga, the practice of either can radically change your life for the better. If there is not time (this is the old excuse) then make time by altering your program, trim the fat from the schedule to make time, not just for meditation and relaxation but also for love (it's all you need, as Mr Lennon tried to tell us). Quality time with the family, hugs, kisses, games and laughter are second to none, and amazingly they are all free.

## Charity: Not a Coat You Wear Twice a Year

Try to give love to others via advice, sympathy, a shoulder to lean on and an ear to listen. Try also to go out of your way for others and do it because it is right, not because there is a profit in it for you, it must be freely and unselfishly given.

This charity starts at home. I know people who would do anything, and I mean absolutely anything on this earth, for their friends down the pub, but they won't shift a muscle for their wife or family. Charity begins at home; if you have more energy and time that's lovely, help others as well. After your kindness, don't go and tell the world about it. Charity, whenever possible, should be a feeling in your heart not a medal on your chest. It is often said that the only real charity is anonymous. I know anonymity is not always possible, but if you have a choice then make it so.

I could give you a page or two in here about how to meditate but I won't because I couldn't do it justice in these few pages, my advice is to go and learn how to do it properly from an expert. Look in the phone book, or on the wall at the library. You'll find a class and it does work, it will be well worth the effort.

## Have a Break

Other ways to relax are holidays. I know this is what the doctor always used to say to my mum when she was bad, 'you need a holiday!' like they were free or something. He might as well have said to my mum 'fly to the moon' for all the good that it did her. She couldn't afford it and the advice was wasted. I include it here because if you can afford it then it's good advice, do it, it is absolutely great therapy, it's a great chance for the brain to recuperate.

Sometimes a good break is all you need. If you can't afford it, I understand that, you'll have to find another method of relaxing, but if you possibly can, please do it.

## Food

Food is a very personal matter but one thing I do know is that light and healthy eating is one of the secrets to longevity, so if you can eat healthily, it's a real bonus. You are what you eat, if you eat rubbish don't expect to get a grand prix performance. Diet is the ultimate discipline and it took me many years to get a grip on it, so I won't tell you that it'll be easy. If it was easy no one would be fat and people wouldn't be making millions publishing books on diet. What I will say is that what we eat is the most fundamental part of who we are so we should all make it our job to find out more about our food than directions to the nearest Greasy Egg Café. I am by no means an expert on diet, so to increase your knowledge on food go to the professionals. Also listen to what your own body tells you about the food you eat (if it says 'fry-up' or 'Mars Bar' ignore it).

Earlier in the book I listed certain foods that can disturb sleep and trigger adrenalin. Try to avoid them if you can, if you can't, be moderate. Try not to eat too late at night if you want a restful sleep, avoid too much alcohol and smoking at night also, they're stimulants that can trigger adrenalin. Sweets are also the enemy for the same reason. Other substances like cola, red wine, chocolate and cheese contain stimulants, as do many drugs and medicines.

If you ever feel unsure about the contents of your medicine ask your doctor. Appetite suppressants, certain painkillers, asthma inhalers and antidepressants are some other examples.

## Regular Exercise

I know I've already mentioned exercise, but I think it is a very important point so here are some of the benefits of a good workout:

It releases trapped (Rogue) Stress Hormones

Strengthens the heart and lungs

Allows more oxygen to all organs helping them to work more efficiently

Helps prevent obesity by burning calories

Lowers cholesterol

Improves concentration and memory because more oxygen is pumped to the brain

Improves your sex life

Improves self-image and self-esteem

Stimulates endorphin releases (our natural morphine)

Increases stamina and builds resistance to fatigue

Improves mood

Builds muscle, strengthens bones and helps retain nutrients

Lowers blood pressure

Reduces risk of heart attack

Encourages better sleep patterns

A study of healthy adults showed that exercise reduced hostility (the biggest cause of heart attack) by 60% and depression by 30%.

## Chapter Fourteen
# Professional Help

For those who feel they might need a little more help and advice please don't hesitate to go for professional assistance. It can make a positive difference. My mum went to several meetings with other sufferers who were struggling with stress. The information they were given made a huge difference to her quality of life. Being given the tools to fight stress gave her back the control she felt she'd lost.

Like many people, myself included, she felt that her depressions, brought on by stress, came and went at will and she had no control over them. Her new-found knowledge changed all that and she started to take charge of her life once again.

There seems to be a stigma attached to asking for medical assistance when it comes to stress, and there shouldn't be. Asking for help doesn't mean you have failed, it simply means you need more information. If we pick up a virus most of us would have no problem at all in going to the doctor for antibiotics. But as soon as an illness involves the mind, we believe people are going to think badly of us if we go to see a doctor.

Outside of the NHS there are several professional bodies set up to offer advice on stress and depression, for example, the Samaritans, MIND, Relate (if your stress is to do with relationships). The church is also an excellent place to find solace and of course not forgetting the good old GP. Most

GPs these days are pretty clued up on stress-related matters and will be able to offer sound advice and details of local groups which specialise in stress-related problems. All of these invaluable organisations offer excellent counselling, reassurance (it is good to know you are not suffering alone), explanations, encouragement, sympathy and emotional support.

Psychotherapy is also excellent; you can talk out your problems with professionals who'll listen with a knowing and sympathetic ear.

Please don't hesitate to seek help if it is needed, believe me it's a great relief to talk to people who have the answers to your questions and problems. Many people find the solutions to their stress and never suffer again. If you are a little worried, ring up first and ask for advice and information.

# Epilogue
# A Room at the Inn

I see life as being a long journey with what can often be a vague destination. It's often an arduous odyssey littered with obstacles. We often perceive these as impediments to the journey, when in reality they are an imperative. I'd even say they are God-sent; the strength, knowledge and wisdom we acquire when overcoming these stumbling blocks, or tests, are exactly what we need to make our transient goal clear and accessible. Each problem contains its own solution; Deepak Chopra tells us that all problems contain a seed of opportunity for the creation of something new and beautiful, and every problem or problematic person becomes our teacher.

Every rock we move on that craggy road allows us a brighter view of the big picture. The more adversity we meet and overcome, the clearer the goal becomes and the more our limited minds are able to understand and cope as the final destination appears before us.

At the start of the race our consciousness is too immature and weak to carry the trophy that awaits us at the finish line. It is the journey that develops the muscle to carry the metal.

To build a big house you need a big foundation, the bigger the house the bigger the foundation. If you try to build a big house on a small or weak base, the structure will crack and fall. The metaphorical big house that we are talking about is at the end of the journey, the foundation is the schooling we receive, the strength we acquire and the wisdom we develop on the journey. We can't just be given our objective because it's too big for our limited consciousness to hold.

## The Inn

On our journey we find rest spots, inns if you like, where we can rest our weary feet and take respite. These inns are the stopgap jobs we take whilst searching for vocation, the second best we accept until we can locate something worthier.

The problem with these inns is that they often become safe havens, hiding places, permanent shelters from the stormy weather. It is comforting to be out of the wind and rain of life, if only for a short while, but invariably we think to ourselves, 'this is nice, I like it here, I think I'll stay a little bit longer. One more night won't hurt!'

One night at the inn becomes two and two nights three. Suddenly we've been at the inn for so long it becomes less like a rest spot and more like a fixed abode.

Some of us even kid ourselves (or we let others kid us) that the inn is the end of the journey. Others still forget they were on a journey in the first place; though in the dark recesses of their minds a vague recollection keeps trying to surface.

In time the inn becomes anchored to comforts that transform it into a cage. Around the cage are bars of fear; they keep creativity in and creation out. We dare not touch the bars, or even approach them, every time we venture to the periphery of our newly found comfort zone to view the great out side we are pushed back by fear.

The longer we stay, the more comforts we attach. The bars grow thick and become impenetrable.

However, we are not alone at the inn, it is shared by internal and external allies who help us to forget our journey and act as a calming balm for the pain of losing our way. Whilst these allies do offer temporary solace it is conditional, they become enemies should we ever try to leave the inn.

## Internal Allies

Our internal allies, the defence mechanisms, are like unconscious shovels that we employ to bury our pain; we then kid ourselves that where we are is good enough or not our fault or fate, we might even convince ourselves that the inn *is* the destination.

## External Allies

Our external allies are others who have also stayed too long in the inn; we take solace from them and them from us. We quickly learn to attack anyone who tries to leave the inn because if they penetrate the bars of fear, our defences temporarily crumble and we see reality in all its splendour. When this happens we can no longer hide from truth.

## Pain is Transient

Every time we try to leave the inn we feel pain and we associate this pain with everything beyond the bars. We feel that it is a permanent fixture on the outside. Paradoxically we associate comfort with all that is on the inside. Eventually we stop trying to leave.

But the pain is not permanent, it is transient, it only exists on the periphery of the cage and once penetrated the pain dissipates and empowerment begins.

Our internal defences try to protect us from reality by offering valid reasons for staying, our external allies protect themselves from the pain of being reminded that they too should be on the journey by attacking those that try to leave, and destroying the credibility of those that have left.

Comfort consolidates if it isn't regularly challenged. The longer you stay at the inn, the harder it is to leave.

If you have to rest make it fleeting and don't allow too many comforts to grow around you, comforts become milestones when you want to recommence the journey.

## Where Are You Going?

Where you want to be in life is where you should be going; goals are there to be achieved not debated. Whatever it is you want from life 'make it so.' Obstacles are there to make you strong, don't procrastinate over them or fall into the victim mentality ('Oh, poor old me, so many obstacles'). If you are getting more obstacles than most then I'd say you're lucky, it means you have a greater propensity to grow. Move the rocks out of your way and get strong and wise doing it. It is only when you lose sight of the goal that the hurdles loom large, and the opportunities suddenly become impediments.

## Be Grateful for Every Opportunity

If you want to be a painter or an actor or a writer or whatever it is you frame in your minds' eye, why aren't you doing it, or at the very least, why aren't you starting the journey? Because it's too hard? Too many things in the way? Too many other commitments? If it was easy the world would be full of high achievers. It has to be hard, that's the apprenticeship. There is only one person stopping you from being who you want to be, doing what you want to do. You! And that's the only person that you have to change.

Please don't use your influences or your environment as an excuse for failure. It's not them, it is you, if people are trying to stop you from living your life then they're your allies at the inn, they're the hurdles that you have to overcome. If they love you enough they'll grow with you, if you want it enough you'll convince them, if they don't (and you can't) then you'll get left behind.

Once we realise that we are the creators, that we have the ability to create, we'll see that there is nothing we cannot achieve and that all life's problems have seeds of opportunity cocooned within.

Good luck with the journey.

God bless.

Geoff Thompson 2001

# Bibliography

Brady, J. V. (1958), 'Ulcers in 'Executive' Monkeys', *Scientific American* 199 (4), 95–100

Cannon, W. B. (1929), *Bodily Changes in Pain, Hunger, Fear and Rage*, Appleton, New York

Cohen, S. (1973) *Folk Devils and Moral Panics*, Paladin, London

Ellsworth, P. C. and Langer, E. J. (1976), 'Staring and Approach: An Interpretation of the Stare as a Non-specific Activator', *Journal of Personality and Social Psychology* 33, 117–22

Freud, Anna (1968), 'Adolescence', in A. E. Winder and D. L. Angus (eds.), *Adolescence: Contemporary Studies*, American Books, New York

Freud, S. (1920), *Beyond the Pleasure Principle*, 1975 edn, W. W. Norton, New York

Friedman, M. and Rosenman, R. H. (1974), *Type A Behaviour*, Alfred A. Knopf, New York

Holmes, D. S. (1974), 'Investigation of Repressions: Differential Recall of Material Experimentally or Naturally Associated with Ego Threat', *Psychological Bulletin* 81, 632–53

Kobasa, S.C. (1979), 'Stressful Life Events, Personality and Health: An Inquiry into Hardiness', *Journal of Personality and Social Psychology*, 37, 1–11

Lazarus, R. (1980), 'Thoughts on the Relations between Cognition and Emotion', *American Psychologist* 37, 1019–24

Lord F. A, *Civil War Collector's Encyclopaedia*

Meichenbaum, D. and Cameron, R. (1983), 'Stress Inoculation Training: Toward a General Paradigm for Training Coping Skills', In D. Meichenabaum and M. E. Jaremko (eds.), *Stress Reduction and Prevention,* 115–154, Plenum, New York

Rosenam, R. H. et al. (1975), 'Coronary Heart Disease in the Western Collaborative Ground Study: Final Follow-up Experience at 8 and a half Years', *Journal of the American Medical Association* 233, 872–7

Seligman, M. E. P. (1975), *Helplessness: On Depression, Development and Death*, C. A. Freeman, San Francisco

Seligman, M. E. P. and Maier, S. F. (1967), 'Failure to Escape Traumatic Shock', *Journal of Experimental Psychology* 74, 1–9

Selye, H. (1976), *The Stress of Life*, McGraw-Hill, New York

Seyle, H. (1974), *Stress Without Distress*, Lippincott, Philadelphia

Solomon, G. F. (1969), 'Emotions, Stress, The CNS and Immunity', *Annals of the New York Academy of Sciences* 164, 335–43

Stone, A. A. and Neale, J. M. (1984b), 'The Effects of Severe Daily Events on Mood', *Journal of Personality and Social Psychology* 46, 137–144

Stone, A. A. and Neale, J.M. (1984a), 'New Measure of Daily Coping: Developments and Preliminary Results', *Journal of Personality and Social Psychology* 46, 892–906

Thomas, M. H. et al (1977), 'Desensitisation to Betrayals of Real-life Aggression as a Function of Exposure to Television Violence', *Journal of Personality and Social Psychology* 35, 450–8

Weiss, J. M. (1972), 'Psychological Factors in Stress and Disease', *Scientific American* 226 (6), 104–13

Wolp, J. (1958), *Psychotherapy by Reciprocal Inhibition*, Stanford University Press, California

Wortman & Lehman, D. R. (1985), 'Reactions of Life Crises: Support Attempts that Fail', in I. G. Sarason (eds.), *Social Support: Theory, Research and Applications*, 463–489

1. Unfortunately, modern armies, using Pavlovian and operant conditioning, have developed sophisticated ways of overcoming this instinctive aversion. Hence in the Korean War, about 50 per cent of soldiers were willing to fire their weapons, in Vietnam that figure rose to over 90 per cent. The psychological cost for soldiers, as witnessed by the increase in Post-Traumatic Stress Disorder, has been devastating.

2. The dehumanisation and desensitisation involved watching video footage of enemy soldiers acting out atrocities; killing, butchering and raping women and children, until the American soldiers no longer saw their enemy as human beings, rather they viewed them as animals. When they shot at the Viet Cong they felt they were merely shooting rats on a riverbank.

3. The length of time that Rogue Stress Hormones stay in the body (if they are not behaviourally released) before they naturally dissipate is difficult to ascertain, it tends to vary from individual to individual. But it is likely to be a couple of days before they exit naturally or work their way out of the body. If you are suffering from long-term stress the body is probably never free from adrenalin.

4. I am aware that there are other factors involved here and that sexual rebuttal does trigger other psychological aspects like the ego and the superego. I will talk about that in a later chapter.

# THE ELEPHANT AND THE TWIG

## The Art Of Positive Thinking

**14 Golden Rules to Success and Happiness**

GEOFF THOMPSON

SUMMERSDALE

The Elephant and the Twig

The Art Of Positive Thinking

Geoff Thompson

£12.99

Have you ever heard the story of The Elephant and The Twig? In India they train obedience in young elephants (to stop them from escaping) by tying them to a huge immovable object, like a tree, when they are still very young. The tree is so large that no matter how hard the baby elephant pulls and tugs it cannot break free. This develops what is known as 'learned helplessness' in the creature. After trying so hard and for so long to break the hold, only to be thwarted time and again, it eventually believes that, no matter what it does, it cannot escape.Ultimately, as a fully-grown adult weighing several tons, they can tie it to a twig and it won't escape, in fact it won't even try.

Do you ever feel like this? That you are tied to an immovable object and can't break free? That you couldn't possibly give that presentation at work, that you would never be able to go it alone in business, or that you have to remain stuck in a social and lifestyle rut as there is no other alternative? This book shows you that, when it comes down to it, what ties you and prevents you from realising your potential is only a 'twig'.

Geoff Thompson, renowned martial artist and author of *Bouncer*, *Watch My Back* and *On the Door*, guides you through the process of breaking the negative thinking that binds us all and helps you to take the plunge and properly take on life.

# THE GREAT ESCAPE

## The 10 Secrets to Loving your Life and Living your Dreams

GEOFF THOMPSON

author of *The Elephant and the Twig*

SUMMERSDALE

The Great Escape

The 10 Secrets to Loving your Life and Living your Dreams

Geoff Thompson

£12.99

If you feel imprisoned in your job, a relationship or, even worse, if you feel trapped in your life, then this book – the sequel to *The Elephant and the Twig* by bestselling author Geoff Thompson – is definitely for you. It offers the 10 secrets to loving your life and living your dreams and helps you make the Great Escape from where you are to where you would love to be. You can be anything, you can do anything and you can go anywhere. You are a creator with the magic to create whatever you want from your short stay on this spinning planet, but there is a process that must be observed and a path to follow; this book unveils the secrets to both. But be careful, don.t pick up this book unless you are ready to succeed, because once you have read the 10 secrets there will be nothing standing between you and your wildest dreams.

The author has used these secrets to take himself from a bedsit in Coventry where he worked as a floor sweeper in a factory to a *Sunday Times* bestselling writer (with over 20 published books), a West End fight choreographer (*Hard Fruit* at the Royal Court Theatre), a playwright (*One Sock*) and a world renowned martial arts teacher.

Fear – The Friend of Exceptional People

Techniques in Controlling Fear

Geoff Thompson

£12.99

Don't let fear hold you back from achieving everything you want to – let Geoff Thompson, author of *Watch My Back* and *The Elephant and the Twig*, show you how to make fear your friend. Once a doorman at some of Britain's roughest nightclubs and now a world-renowned martial artist, Geoff Thompson has had more to be frightened of than most. Here he shares his secrets for overcoming your fears to help you live life to the max. From spiders to public speaking, job interviews to physical conflict, Geoff takes you through proven techniques of combating whatever it is you're afraid of.

- Understand your physical reactions to fear and how they can be used to your advantage

- Overcome the negative feelings that make you think you can't succeed

- Learn methods to defeat your fears with Geoff's unique Fear Pyramid system

- Achieve your full potential without worries restricting you

Geoff has included interviews with people from the SAS and the boxing circuit to inspire you to believe that nothing should hold you back from living your dreams.

GEOFF THOMPSON

WATCH MY BACK

'I train for the first shot
– it's all I need.'

'LENNIE MCLEAN HAD THE BRAWN, DAVE COURTNEY HAD THE
CHARM, BUT GEOFF THOMPSON IS IN A CLASS OF HIS OWN' FHM

## Watch My Back

### Geoff Thompson

### £12.99

'A brilliant insight!'
**Reggie Kray**

'This man is very, very hard.
Buy his book if you know what's good for you.'
**Maxim**

'This is as real as it gets.'
**Dave Courtney**

'The psyche-outs, the stabbings, glassings, incidents
involving the camaraderie of the door . . .
Thompson's 300 fights – never losing, not once
– are recorded in this excellent book.'
**Loaded**

'Surviving 300 bloody confrontations and earning the
fearsome reputation as a knockout specialist,
Thompson takes you as close to real-life street fights
as you'll ever want to get.'
**Bizarre Magazine**

'A compelling insight.'
**Arena**

'Utterly compelling . . . read it.'
**Men's Fitness**

'Grabs you by the throat and doesn't put you down.'
**Front**

GEOFF THOMPSON

BESTSELLING AUTHOR OF 'WATCH MY BACK'

RED MIST

# Red Mist

## Geoff Thompson

'I was dangerous because I had nothing to lose.' Martin is a man disillusioned with life, and with good reason. Coming from a broken home where violence was the norm, he lives alone in a squalid flat, working as a brickie when he can. The monotony of his existence is dramatically altered when he meets the beautiful Ginger, who is desperately trying to escape from Mick, her obsessive boyfriend and brutal tormentor. Keeping Ginger out of harm's way means putting his life on the line as Martin becomes sucked into an underworld of drugs and violence, where arguments are settled with a fist or a bullet. Gripping, honest, brutal and raw.

Geoff Thompson pulls no punches in this explosive first novel.

www.summersdale.com